The Reluctant Networker

Giving you the tools
and confidence to give
networking a go

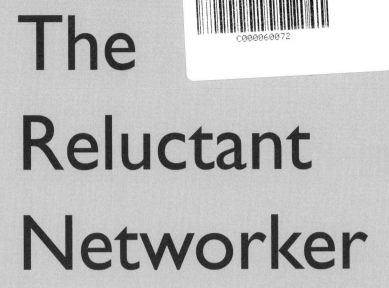

Neil Munz-Jones

© Neil Munz-Jones

ISBN: 978-1-906316-50-1

All rights reserved.
Published in 2010 by HotHive Books
www.thehothive.com

The right of Neil Munz-Jones to be identified as the author of this work has been asserted by him in accordance with the Copyright, Designs and Patents Act 1988.

A CIP record of this book is available from the British Library.
No part of this publication may be reproduced in any form or by any means without permission from the copyright holder.

Printed in the UK by TJ International, Padstow.

"Never be afraid to try something new.

Remember, amateurs built the Ark.

Professionals built the Titanic"

Anon

Acknowledgements

With many thanks to the following Reluctant and Natural Networkers for all their support, ideas and advice:

Richard Ball	Peter Fisk	Bhavick Morjaria
Ian Barnes	Mark Fritz	Laura Olver
Helen Bass	Steve Goodburn	Karan Paige
Charmian Caines	Sue Grist	John Purkiss
Ian Cheshire	Mark Hart	Peter Russell
Rashid Chinchanwala	Stephen Hooker	June Sebley
Mike Cutt	Christopher Humphry	Karen Swinden
Charmaine Damley-Jones	David Jackson	Paul von Kesmark
Ed Daubeney	Tim Kruger	Joëlle Warren
Charlie Dawson	Jonathan Mardall	Ian Williams
Fionnuala Duggan	Jo McFarland	Andrew Woodward

About the author

Neil is a Director of MDJ^2 Consulting, a company he founded in 2005 to specialise in Strategy, Category Management, Organisation Design and M&A for the Retail sector. Despite being a Reluctant Networker he wins all his business via networking. Prior to that he spent several years in Director roles in the international DIY/Home Improvement sector at Kingfisher/B&Q and one of its suppliers, Caradon. Neil has a BA (Hons) from Oxford University and an MBA from INSEAD. In 2008 Neil published a case study "You Can Do It If You B&Q It" in conjunction with Professor Nitin Sanghavi at Manchester Business School (MBS) and he teaches at MBS using the case study. Neil is married and has three sons.

Contents

Introduction 8

Chapter 1:   Four good **Reasons** why you should network 22

1   *Networking is a key way to get many of the best jobs* 26
2   *Networking is a great sales tool* 30
3   *Networking can help make a success of your current role or project* 32
4   *Networking can help increase your long-term career options.* 34

Chapter 2:   **Principles** of good networking 38

1   *Change your mindset…we network all the time* 41
2   *Develop a style that works for you* 43
3   *Effective networkers build long-term relationships based on trust* 45
4   *Know your strengths and play to them; do what you enjoy and are good at* . . 47
5   *Tap into your network's networks* 49
6   *It is a two-way thing; give as well as take* 51
7   *Keep high standards.* 53
8   *Do it while you do not 'need' anything.* 55

Chapter 3:   **Practical Tips** for The Reluctant Networker 58

1   *Have a database* 61
2   *Join a limited number of the networking websites and networking groups* . . . 62

3   Focus on what you want and who you network with 65

4   Communicate using all media 72

5   If you 'want' something from your networking be prepared and make it easy
    for people to help you 81

6   It is never too late to get back in touch 83

7   Find a reason to keep in touch, call or go and see people 87

8   If you are going to go to networking events, make the most of them 88

9   You'll need to network with both men and women 92

10 Learn from other networking styles 98

11 Expect lots of no's, delays, cancellations, 'fruitless' meetings...it's not personal...
    polite persistence works 99

Chapter 4: **How to get started** 106

1   Out of a job and looking for a new role 111

2   Networking when your job requires it 113

3   Starting to network when you are in a job 115

Chapter 5: **Why should I help?**
    Because I can...most people are keen to help. 122

Introduction

Who should read this?

You should read the book if you can answer 'yes' to any of the following statements:
- I have a job but want to see what else is out there in case I want to move companies.
- I have a job but am worried that I might lose it.
- I don't have a job at the moment and need to find one.
- I am a freelancer (in any field/sector) and need a new project or want to generate some new leads for future business.
- I have a job and have realised that I could be more effective if I had a network of contacts I could call on to be better informed or to help me solve problems.
- I have a job and have realised that networking can help me develop my career in the long-term... but I am not really sure how to get started, especially as I have so little free time to do it.

If you think that networking could help your career but also that you are not great at it you should read this book. You may assume that you are not an accomplished networker because you don't enjoy spending your free time going to networking events or breakfasts. By the end of the book you should realise that you don't have to spend vast amounts of time at these networking events to be a very effective networker.

The 'obvious' answer to who should read this is people who are looking for a new job, project or opportunity (at any level and type of role) and do not want to rely just on newspaper adverts, job websites and head hunters or recruitment agencies. It is especially relevant if you are the type of person that does not enjoy calling up 'friends of friends' or cold calling senior people in companies where you would like to work. Or maybe you are someone who keeps putting off getting in touch with a former colleague who may be able to help you because 'he/she won't remember me' or 'why would they want to hear from me after all these years?'

What if you have been made redundant? How are you going to explain why you left your past company without feeling awkward? So you keep putting off opportunities to go and meet new contacts. It's safer and more 'comfortable' to rely on job adverts and recruitment agencies. At least there is a job up for grabs, and so there is less likelihood of failure or rejection (fear of both of which is a common and understandable emotion after redundancy).

But this book is not just for people looking for jobs. Maybe you have already realised that networking is a good idea for long-term career success. A survey by Roffey Park Management Institute (*The Future of Careers*) highlighted 'being a networker' a key competency for a successful career (the others were 'being an expert' and 'being self-reliant and emotionally resilient'). The trouble is that you think you are not very good at it. Perhaps you think you are shy and find meeting new people quite difficult. The thought of 'working a room' at a networking event brings you out in a cold sweat. Calling up contacts and meeting them to see if you can help each other might sound like a good idea but is not really your style. If only you could get some tips to get started that are relatively easy and do not take up too much time.

What if you have set up your own business (as I did) and have realised that without a 'big company' name behind you, networking is the only way to win any business? The freedom of having your own business is great, but selling can be much tougher. Unless you tell people about yourself and your business, you won't get many calls.

I have been through all these situations and have experienced many of these emotions, which is why I have written this book. I am a 'Reluctant Networker' and have met many people whose response goes something along the lines of 'oh yes, that's me too!'

What is a Reluctant Networker?

There is no Oxford English Dictionary (O.E.D.) definition (yet!) but it goes something like this. You are someone that realises or has been told that networking is a good thing but you do not find it a 'natural' act.

Some common traits might be:
- You would rather watch paint dry than go to a networking event where you will not know anyone and are meant to 'work the room'.
- You prefer email to the telephone for contacting new people or ones you do not know well.
- Some of your colleagues are always on their mobile phones in between meetings, listening to lots of messages and then calling back; your phone may be more than a fashion accessory but you are unlikely to have it glued to your ear all the time.
- You tend only to keep in touch with your contacts when you have something specific to talk about.

- You are not great at keeping in touch with former colleagues.
- When you have a quiet moment, you tend to catch up on your reading rather than call people to chat about how things are going.
- You probably think you are shy (even if others may perceive you to be outgoing).

The great news is that, although I am a Reluctant Networker, I have realised that it is not as difficult as many people think and it can even be fun! Most of my networking is done on a one-to-one basis, which I really enjoy. As a result I have been able to build my new business via networking.

The really positive lesson for me has been that there is a whole world of people out there, willing to help. As my former mentor said when I asked him why he gave up so much time to help me, "The age of altruism is not dead." All we have to do is ask and make it easy for people to give you that help.

So, as the table on the next page shows, 'Reluctant Networkers' can be just as effective as 'Natural Networkers', i.e. the people with a huge network of active contacts that seem to be always on the phone and attending endless networking breakfasts and evenings.

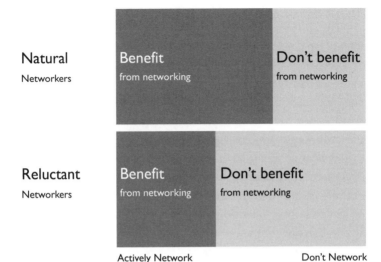

	Actively Network	Don't Network
Natural Networkers	**Benefit** from networking	**Don't benefit** from networking
Reluctant Networkers	**Benefit** from networking	**Don't benefit** from networking

From the conversations with people in my network I am convinced that there are more Reluctant than Natural Networkers. Sathnam Sanghera wrote in *The Times* in an article on networking: "For every confident networker there are probably thousands who feel allergic to the idea, on the grounds that it sounds cold and predatory and brings to mind gruesome images of people cutting you dead because someone more important has drifted into view." But I know enough of these Reluctant Networkers to know that many of them have figured out a way to benefit from networking. So it is not just the Natural Networkers that can benefit from networking (and not all of them do benefit, by the way).

What networking is and is not

One of the O.E.D.'s definitions of a network is "a chain of interconnected persons". Networking for me is all about using this chain to achieve my career goals and needs. 'Using' the chain does not mean it is all one way traffic. I spend a lot of time helping others too. A lot of people assume that networking is about going to 'networking events', joining 'networking groups' that meet on a regular basis or signing up to internet-based networking databases. Many people find all or some of these activities quite difficult and not very useful. Therefore they assume that they cannot network, or that they are no good at it. All of these activities are a *means* to an end, they are not the *end* in itself. There are many different ways to network and you will need to find the ones that work for you.

Another misconception about networking, especially amongst Reluctant Networkers, is that networking is somehow an unpleasant activity, (i.e. it is a politically correct word used to 'legitimise' using people to get what you want.) The reality is that people use networking all the time and it is what makes a lot of businesses tick. One of the principles referred to later in the book is that 'It's a two-way thing'. So it is not just about using other people to get what you want, it is more about helping each other out to your mutual benefit. When you think of it that way and see how you yourself can help others, it does not feel so bad asking for help when you need it. If it was all one way, I doubt it would be very effective because the people being 'used' would give up pretty quickly.

In essence, I believe that you need to think of networking as a lifelong approach to 'doing business', rather than a one-off activity in order to 'find a job' (though it really can help you find one).

The advice of one of my contacts was, "it's not something you turn on and off like a tap, it's more a way of life." I started out when in a bit of a crisis, as I needed a job, but soon realised that successful networkers do it all the time. I am now convinced that the successful ones rarely have these crises, or they are short-lived when they do occur.

So do not think that networking is just about finding a job. For many people it is how they win business. A colleague has a successful consulting business and claims he has never done any selling. He invests time in networking and finds that people keep calling him and giving him work. Not only does he not need to sell, but he has to turn business down. For others it is a great way to be the best informed on what is going on in their industry and so helping them to be successful in their current jobs. As a business consultant I use my network all the time to help me deliver successful projects.

Because the purpose of this book is to help people increase their long-term career options, the emphasis is on 'business' rather than 'social' networking, even though the two can be connected. It is also focused on 'external' rather than 'internal' networking, i.e. networking primarily with people working in organisations other than one's own. This is not to suggest that 'internal' networking is not important… far from it, with more and more business articles being written about the need for excellent 'internal' networking skills to be successful within a large organisation. Of course, success in your current role is always a good way to increase your options in the long run.

Why you should read this book

I believe that networking can help you get control of your career and increase your options. The book is packed full of practical tips on how to network more effectively, written from the 'Reluctant Networker' perspective. Here is a bit about my own experience and why I believe this to be the case.

Firstly the impressive bit: I have a degree from Oxford University and an MBA from one of Europe's leading business schools, INSEAD in France. I used to be the Managing Director of a £30m manufacturing business with 300 employees, selling products all over the world. In another role I was the Programme Director of the post-merger integration of the French company Castorama following a £3bn hostile takeover by Kingfisher, the leading British retailer. You can imagine the reception we got at the start in France as those nice, friendly Brits who have just taken us over... I have worked directly for three CEOs of some of Britain's largest, quoted companies and I speak four languages pretty well.

Why all this trumpet-blowing? Because you might think that with all those qualifications my business career has been a bit of a breeze. The reality is that it has not been straightforward. I have been made redundant twice. Until the end of 2005 I had only ever worked for large companies, but had dreamt of having my own business. In June 2005 I went to Venice with my wife to celebrate our 40th birthdays. Whilst we were there I wrote some goals for my 40s, the first of which was: "Get control of my career" (see **Practical Tip 3** on page 65 for more on goal-setting, as this is easier said than done for many of us).

I really have used networking as a means to get back control of my career. I now have my own consulting company, I have had a Business School case study published, I lecture and have written this book. I love being in control of my own destiny, the variety of my work as well as getting to take longer holidays at a time of *my* choice, not when my boss allows me to.

I have wanted to write for many years but have never had the time or known what to write about. The good thing about adversity is that you can learn a lot from it. My response to redundancy nine years ago when I left manufacturing was to start networking. The thought of doing this really did not fill me with joy; I had assumed wrongly that it meant cold calling people and asking them for a job. I had only ever got jobs via head hunters, but rapidly realised that they would only find me other manufacturing jobs that would require endless rounds of restructuring and cost-cutting, none of which I really enjoyed.

Several years on, I could not run my consulting business successfully without networking… that is how I win all my business. I have used my network to help me write this book and it really has been a great example of the power of one's network. Some of the examples are stories from other people's experiences that bring to life the principles and tips in the book. Some of the tips themselves have come from conversations with people in my network. And these conversations have also reinforced my view that there are many Reluctant Networkers out there! Everybody I have spoken to has been able to contribute in some way and make it a better book as a result.

But I don't just 'gain' from networking. As I'll explain in **Principle 6** on page 51 – *'It's a two-way thing.'* You have to 'give' as well, and I devote a fair amount of networking time to helping people who have approached me. I have talked to a lot of friends and colleagues who have also been made redundant or wanted to change careers and not known how to go about it. After a few lunches, coffees or drinks with them, I realised that I had acquired a lot of experience and helpful tips.

So, after much encouragement from my wife, I have put this all down on paper. There are already plenty of books on networking, some good, some less so. But none take the perspective of the Reluctant Networker, admitting that what makes total sense in theory is actually very hard to do when it requires changing one's behaviour. General Norman Schwarzkopf said: "The truth of the matter is that you always know the right thing to do – the hard part is doing it." These tips are very practical and there are no complex theories, models or frameworks here. They are based on my own experiences and on talking to many friends and colleagues about what they have learnt. Most of it is simple and fairly obvious, but I know that it is often hard to stand back and reflect. This is particularly true if you are going through a major transition such as trying to find a new job.

I have had a lot of input and feedback from my friends and colleagues (see Acknowledgements on page 4). I am particularly grateful to my wife Charmaine, Rashid Chinchanwala, Mark Hart, David Jackson, Jonathan Mardall, Bhavick Morjaria and Peter Russell, who have given me lengthy and useful feedback in pulling this together.

Read on and think about how it could help you in your career. Chapter 4 on how to get started will help you take those vital first steps. Please do not assume that you need to follow all the suggestions to become a better networker. We all have different ways of interacting with other people, so use the tips that you find helpful. This is about changing your behaviours, which can be quite difficult. So maybe start by picking one or two of the suggestions that you find most helpful and easy to do. This is particularly true if you are already in a job and do not have much free time to start networking.

Good luck and please do get in touch via www.reluctantnetworker.com if you have any other tips or networking successes you would like to share.

Summary

Who should read it?

♦ Anyone who has realised that networking could help their career but thinks that they are not very good at it or that 'networking is not for me'.

What is a Reluctant Networker?

Someone who should read this book! You probably:
♦ Don't enjoy going to networking events.
♦ Don't like using the phone to call new contacts or re-connect with old ones.
♦ Are not great at keeping in touch with former colleagues.

What networking is and is not

♦ You need to think of networking as a means to an end. Attending networking events or calling up new contacts are both networking activities that you may (or may not) enjoy. There are plenty of other ways to network that Reluctant Networkers may find easier to do, such as meeting up with people on a one-to-one basis.

- For me the 'end' is to use my network to maintain control of my career and allow me to do what I enjoy and am good at.
- Think of networking as a lifelong approach to doing business, not something to be turned on and off when you need something... and that means 'giving' as well as 'taking'.

Why should you read this book?

Reluctant Networkers can be very *effective* networkers.
The book will:
- Change the way you think about networking.
- Give you lots of practical tools and techniques.
- Show you how to get started.

All written from the perspective of a Reluctant Networker.

Chapter 1:

Four good reasons why you should network and how it can help

"Networking is an essential part of

building wealth"

Armstrong Williams

(US political commentator)

Why you should network and how it can help

Networking is a great way to increase your career options, which puts you firmly in control. When I left the manufacturing business back in 2001, I realised that networking was the only way for me to get what I wanted. Otherwise my career was being dictated by recruitment agencies and their clients, deciding how suitable I was for a particular role. Because of my previous experience I was being limited to roles in the manufacturing sector. By networking I managed to move into another sector and so open up a whole new avenue of career choices.

Networking can:

♦ Help you access many of the best roles that otherwise would not have been available to you by sticking to more traditional means of job search.

♦ Give you the chance to run your own business, by using your network to drive your sales and marketing efforts.

♦ Increase your chances of success in your current role, by benefiting from the knowledge, experience and contacts in your network.

♦ Increase your long-term career options for two reasons: firstly it can help ensure you are considered for roles, even when you are not actively looking for one; secondly, as large organisations shy away from more mature workers, you can use your network to build a new 'portfolio' career with diverse sources of income.

1 Networking is a key way to get many of the best jobs

In his book *From New Recruit to High Flyer*, Hugh Karseras writes about the need for an effective network: "Naïve is the person who thinks that career and job opportunities are solely a function of merit. Merit counts for nothing unless the right people know about you. As one executive says: 'You have to put your name out there. If people are talking about you, it creates opportunities.'"

Although many people tend to think that the best way to find a new job is to look in the papers, talk to head hunters and use websites, the reality is that this is not how most jobs are filled. I asked a number of outplacement consultants for their experiences and was told that on average only 5–10% of jobs filled by external candidates are found via adverts; a further 15–20% of jobs are filled via head hunters or recruitment agencies; this means that up to 70% are filled via networking and direct approaches to companies. This is backed up by a *Times* article on networking in August 2007 that claimed that, according to the American Bureau of Labour Statistics, 75% of executives get their position through contacts. These are the jobs that you never hear about until they are already filled. So this latter area is what we should be concentrating on – and getting better at it in terms of the techniques we use and developing our self-confidence to do it well.

I asked a few business contacts how they had got their jobs and for stories about other people's successful networking. A friend wanted to go and live in the Channel Islands where he had grown up. He talked to a few school friends when back visiting one holiday. As a result he got a job as a member of the senior management team of one of the Channel Islands' biggest companies. This is a good example of using networking to take control to fulfil a career and lifestyle objective. He found the role via networking even though there was a recruitment agency looking for candidates. Neither had they found him, nor did he know that they were handling the search. Another person got his job as a result of his grandmother talking to her neighbour over the garden hedge about his looking for a job... the neighbour recruited the grandson! Someone else recruited the father of one of her sons' classmates, having only met through school. If you ask your friends how they got their jobs, I'm sure you'll come across a few similar stories.

The reality is that some career moves are easier than others:

3. Different role, same sector
Medium risk
Try and make the move within your company first. Networking can help too.

4. Different role, different sector
High risk
Networking probably the only way to make this kind of move.

1. Current role, current company.

2. Same role, different company in same or different sector
Low risk
Use both traditional means (head hunters, press, online) and networking.

This is a similar concept to the one written about in *What Colour is Your Parachute?* To give an example, assume you are a marketing manager for a consumer products business and want to do a similar role but in a different consumer products company because you want a new challenge. In this case you want to move from Box 1 to Box 2 above. The more 'traditional' methods of finding another job such as press and online adverts or head hunters and recruitment agencies should usually work. Nevertheless networking with former colleagues will probably open up more opportunities for you.

However, what if you want to change functional roles? What if you are a finance manager of a consumer products business and want to move into a marketing role (Box 1 to Box 3)? Or what if you are a finance manager in a manufacturing business and fancy a change of both role (into marketing) and sector (away from manufacturing and into consumer products) i.e. moving to Box 4? In these cases, the more traditional means of finding a job are less likely to work.

This is because there are usually hundreds of applicants, many of whom already have the relevant skills and experience. So the company does not have to take a risk on someone with a different skill set trying to change role. I have spoken to a number of head hunters about this. They say that even when clients ask them to add a few 'wild card' candidates onto the shortlist, the client almost always ends up offering the role to the tried and tested candidates. Companies tend to be risk-averse.

Therefore the higher the 'risk' in your proposed move, the more likely you are to secure it via networking. I moved from a role running a medium-sized manufacturing business to leading an international post-merger integration of two retail companies (i.e Box 1 to Box 4 above). Had the company used a head hunter and recruited externally, I would not even have made it onto a shortlist as I had never done a post-merger integration before. I secured it because I had worked at the company for three years almost a decade earlier and had kept up my contacts after leaving. When I read about the acquisition I approached them to do some consultancy work and they ended up offering me a full-time role as an employee. This is a great example of why you should always keep in touch with former colleagues (see **Practical Tip 3** on page 65 – 'Focus on who you network with').

Another point to consider is that using recruitment agencies or head hunters is expensive for companies; they will charge the company between 25% and 33% of your starting salary to find you. Given that people are moving roles so much more frequently, recruitment costs can really add up. Networking does not cost the company these fees. In an article in the FT in April 2007 called "Social Networking hits the workplace", it reported that almost half of UK employers offer their employees incentives if they recruit someone introduced by an existing employee; needless to say, the incentives are a lot less than the head hunters' fees (the article quoted one company offering an incentive of between £1,000 and £7,000 depending on the level of seniority of the recruited candidate, another between £2,000 and £10,000) and shows the value many companies are putting on networking. The article also quoted an HR Director: "In the UK employee referrals bring in 20% of our recruits at 50% cost savings." As another example, the major consulting firms actively promote their 'Hire a friend' schemes as their employees can judge the 'cultural fit' of a potential employee, and candidates will often be fast-tracked through first-round interviews.

A side aspect of networking to find a role is that it can make 'cold calling' a company or new contact a lot easier. Imagine how much more likely you are to get to speak or ideally meet with someone if you have been 'introduced' by someone in your network. If possible get them to email their contact, copying you in on the email, making the introduction. Then you can follow up directly yourself. I guarantee that your odds of a meeting will be significantly higher. Alternatively, ask them for the contact details and their permission to use their name when you call or email. So if you have particular companies or contacts that you'd like to meet, have a list and show them to the people in your network; it is an easy way for them to help you and will make your 'cold calling' much easier. This approach is equally valid if you are trying to get into a company to sell your products, consulting services, etc (see **Principle 2** below).

2 Networking is a great sales tool

As mentioned in the introduction, networking is a critical tool for my consulting business. Apart from repeat business, all my work comes from some sort of networking, as I find this a much more effective selling tool than e.g. cold calling or advertising. Typically my new clients have come from referrals from former bosses, colleagues or other clients. Here is a real example from my experience: I had lunch with a well-connected former boss and told him about my activities and the type of projects I was doing. About two months later I got a call from a new potential client saying that my former boss had given him my name. Two weeks later I was consulting to his company after just a 30-minute telephone interview and have now completed three assignments for them. Three weeks after another meeting with this former boss, I had a call from a charity about a six-month full-time strategy project. We had one thing in common, the same former boss, who again had put us in touch.

Here are some other examples:

One project I worked on started out because the client wanted to benefit from my network of contacts in the retail sector. I was taken on for just four days to arrange meetings with a number of major retailers. In addition to earning a bonus for every meeting I arranged, I ended up working on the project for nine months, all because I had an active network.

I used to work with someone in a large organisation that had many subsidiaries across the UK and Europe. When he left the organisation to go into consulting, one of the first things he did was to draw a 'spider diagram' of all the subsidiaries in our former organisation and all the senior individuals who had worked there. He then added where they worked now and re-established contact with them, especially the ones he considered to be his 'business friends' (see **Practical Tip 3** on page 65 – *Focus on who you network with*'). He has won significant amounts of business from these former colleagues. Even though he dislikes 'selling', he is good at keeping in touch with them by phone and occasional meetings. As a result, they call him when they are 'ready to buy'. As he said, "I don't think I appreciated the value of this network or how to use it. But remember that you have to be 'genuine' when you call and always be on the look out for ways you can help them too, maybe by 'connecting' them with other people."

In all these examples, having an active network was essential as a selling tool to enable us to develop new careers. We were effectively marketing ourselves, which is why using our networks of business relationships and contacts is particularly effective. *The Times* article on networking mentioned in **Reason 1** on page 26 stated: "The Law Society says that the British legal profession gains a fifth of its new business by referral or recommendation." To back this up, the lawyer, accountant and IT support I use for my business have all come via referrals from contacts in my network.

3   Networking can help make a success of your current role

Your network is a hugely powerful source of knowledge, skills, experience and contacts. Why not put it to good effect in ensuring you make a success of your current role? Here are a couple of simple ways to do this.

The first is to help you solve specific challenges:

I have no direct employees but do have a large network of other freelance consultants that I can call on as needed. I have won work on the back of being able to bring these colleagues in to projects where they had particular expertise that I did not have but that the client needed. On a less formal basis I am always calling up people in my network to fill in gaps in my knowledge. Clients expect expertise in all aspects of the project, yet inevitably there will be a few parts where I know a fair bit but am not an expert. My network is invaluable in these circumstances. I also spend quite a bit of time doing the reverse i.e. providing my expertise to people in my network when they call me up and ask for my help (see **Principle 6** on page 51 – 'It's a two-way thing').

A former colleague working in a supply chain role in a large company was given a new project that involved tackling a new set of issues and challenges for both him and the company. There was no experience to call on from his colleagues, so he called up former colleagues to get their insights. He also did a search of the networking website of which he was a member. This enabled him to access new contacts with relevant experience. He was amazed at the willingness of people to help. You can contact total strangers on the basis of being in the same (open access) networking website and ask to pick their brains. These conversations gave him a great start on the project, ensuring he covered all the right issues and knew about the likely pitfalls.

The networking organisation of which I am a member has reported cases where large consulting projects have been entirely resourced by independent consultants who are members of the networking organisation.

In a similar way, I have used my network to help me write this book. I selected a number of my contacts who I thought were Reluctant Networkers and asked them how they went about networking. What tips and real life stories of successful networking could they pass on? The book is much richer for having all their anecdotes and insights.

The second way is less tangible and is all about the power of information:

Many skilled networkers use their contacts to stay ahead of competitors (even colleagues!) in what is really happening in their industries and markets. You don't get the truth and the semi-confidential information out of people you hardly know. Think of it as being like a journalist and how they get their 'off the record' comments. But remember that mutual trust is a key ingredient (see **Principle 3** on page 45 – '*Effective networkers build long-term relationships based on trust*').

What if you want to find out about a potential new customer, supplier, employee or even a company to buy? You do not want to rely solely on information that they tell you themselves. A strong network of contacts built up over time, based on mutual trust will certainly help you elicit the truth before you need to make a decision.

Clearly 'internal' networking within your organisation is critical as well to make a success of your current role. So even though this is not the focus of this book don't forget those 'informal' meetings with colleagues over a cup of coffee, lunch or the water cooler.

4 Networking can help increase your long-term career options

The final reason why you should network is based on taking a long-term view of its benefits. Over the course of your career you will work with many different people (colleagues, customers, suppliers, consultants etc). This network can be put to great use if you manage it carefully:

◆ Be clear about what you are looking for at each stage of your career.
◆ Make the time to stay in touch with people in your network, not just when you need something from them.
◆ Take an interest in them as individuals so that you build personal rapport.
◆ Finally, help them out when you can.

If you do this on a regular basis, viewing it as a long-term investment, I am convinced that it will open up options that you otherwise would not be aware of.

Recently I passed on the CV of a former colleague for a potential role for which he is well-qualified. We worked together over six years ago and have kept in touch since. We try to help each other out whenever we can. Maybe he will not get the job, but if he had not kept in touch with me, I would not have thought of him when I came across the role through the membership of my networking organisation. By chance, he was actively looking for a new role and was extremely grateful that I had alerted him to the opportunity.

The Times publishes 'The Times Power 100', a list of the top 100 most powerful business people in Britain. For each person in the list, it shows their 'connections' with others in the list. In many instances these connections go back many years when they had worked together at different organisations to the ones at which they are now. No doubt they keep in touch and network together when they can. And do not believe that because they have got so far in their careers there are no Reluctant Networkers in their ranks! I have met one or two and know that they would meet some of the criteria of "What is a Reluctant Networker?" in the Introduction (see page 11).

Charles Handy in his book *The Elephant and the Flea: Looking Backwards to the Future*, refers to the changing nature of the British workforce. He wrote that in the Year 2000 only 40% of the workforce was in 'permanent' full-time employment. "By 1996… 67% of British businesses only had one employee, the owner… and in 1994 only 11% of businesses employed more than five people." Large organisations are much less loyal and there are many articles about how it is harder for people over a certain age (usually 50 is mentioned) to find permanent, full-time work in large companies. In addition, with reduced pension benefits it is likely that many of us will have to work longer and we may have to find this work outside of large company, full-time employment for, say, the last 20 years of our working lives.

As Handy writes:
"I told the doubters of the forty-eight year old advertising account executive who was complaining to me that there were no longer any jobs in the ageist advertising world for people like him. Whilst he was talking to me in my home, the electrician repairing our wiring put his head round the door to say that he would be back, but not for a week. 'I'm sorry,' he said, seeing my face darken with disappointment, 'but I've got too many jobs on at the moment.'

"That was the future, I told my account executive; lots of electrician-type jobs, meaning customers and clients for the independent worker, but fewer and fewer of his own type of job where you sold your time in advance, usually years in advance to an organisation."

This world of the 'flea', the independent worker doing lots of different jobs at the same time, is far easier to start if you *already* have an active network, rather than if you have to start building a new one from scratch or reviving an underdeveloped one.

Networking really can help you achieve a number of different things, depending on what your career goals are. The great thing is that once you have the network, it is fairly easy to use it to help you switch careers if your objectives change.

Summary

You can use networking to achieve a number of different objectives:

♦ Use it to find a new job, especially if you are trying to move into a different function or industry from the one you are currently in – remember that up to 70% of jobs are filled via networking or direct approaches to companies. If you only rely on adverts or agencies/head hunters your pool of available jobs is limited and you are missing out on roles you'll never hear about.

♦ Use it to make a success of your current project or role; with a good network you don't need to know all the answers, you just need to know people who can help you fill in the gaps in your knowledge.

♦ Use it to build a career as a freelancer (in many different fields), giving you much greater freedom and control of your life and career. Just like full-time jobs, a lot of these projects do not get advertised; they get filled via the client using their network as they tend not to have the time or the budget to advertise.

♦ Even if you have a secure job and are doing it well, networking can help you increase your long-term options: good networkers are (a) less likely to be out of work and (b) if they ever are out of work, are likely to find a new role more quickly.

Chapter 2:

Principles of good networking

"It is our attitude at the beginning of a difficult task which, more than anything else, will affect its successful outcome"

William James

(American psychologist and philosopher)

1 Change your mindset... we network all the time

We use our network all the time in our daily lives, especially when we want to buy services. How many times have you bought a service based on a friend's recommendation? Plumbers and electricians recommended by friends tend to be more reliable than sticking a pin into the *Yellow Pages* and calling the first few in the book... you could be selecting based on whether their company name starts with a letter early in the alphabet! Why not use networking to find work yourself? The only difference is that in this case you are 'selling' rather than 'buying'. For Reluctant Networkers this can be a *big* difference.

I don't particularly enjoy selling but know that it is a fundamental part of any successful business. A successful salesman friend of mine has a great attitude to selling that he even used when asking girls out on dates! His philosophy is: "Every time I get a 'no', it just means I am one step closer to a 'yes'." He is definitely *not* a Reluctant Networker. But for many of us, fear of rejection looms large and can stop us trying or asking for things we would like. I try and take my friend's approach to selling. Whilst it is not like waving a magic wand, it certainly helps make it easier.

One technique that you could try is to turn the question on its head. If you are thinking of trying something that you find difficult, rather than ask yourself "what if they say 'no'?", ask yourself "what if they say 'yes'?". Then think of all the consequences of a 'yes'. Once you have done that, only then think about the "what if they say 'no'?" outcome and ask yourself how bad that would be in comparison with the consequences of a 'yes'.

In many ways though, networking is not really about selling. Even when you are looking for a job, think of it as unearthing opportunities you did not know about and building your knowledge. You only need to sell yourself when there is an actual job up for grabs. When I first set out to build my network, I dreaded the thought of contacting people I had never met before and putting them under pressure to meet me or to offer me a job. This is where the courses and books on networking get it right. Don't put people under pressure by asking for a job. If somebody thinks they may have to say 'no', they are far less likely to want to meet in the first place. Put them at ease by saying you do not expect them to have a role; you just want to pick their brains for advice and perhaps some suggestions of other people to talk to. Put that way, people are usually flattered to have been asked for their help. Once I had tried this approach a few times, it was amazing how much more I enjoyed networking. Now it was just another good way to meet new people and find out about companies and industries I was already interested in.

Of course, there is an exception to every rule; a good friend of mine has found two roles by ringing up former contacts and asking for a job. But he has known these people *very well* and is excellent at what he does. So I would not recommend this to everybody, but on occasions it may pay to be bold and come right out with what you want!

The other key mindset change is to realise that networking is a two-way thing (see **Principle 6** on page 51). If you do believe it is a lifelong way of doing business, there will be plenty of opportunities for you to help others. So when it is your turn to ask for help, it should be easier to ask, when you know that you can 'give' as well as 'take'.

2   Develop a style that works for you

I know effective networkers that adopt very different approaches. Some are incredibly organised, plan their networking in great detail and then execute their plan with almost military precision. Others are a lot less structured, and are happy as long as they are regularly 'out there' talking to and meeting their network, but with no grand plan behind them. A highly successful entrepreneur neighbour of mine used to do his networking at the pub once or twice a week, where he made and cultivated many interesting local contacts.

There are plenty of people, books and courses telling you the best way to network whilst looking for a job. These will include standard letters, telephone style and technique and what to ask for when in a networking meeting. For example, you may get told that in a networking meeting the objective is, for example, to get three more names for you to contact and not to leave until you have got them! This may not be appropriate and many people feel uncomfortable coming across as too pushy. Similarly, the 'standard' letters to apply for jobs or to ask for a networking meeting may not work for you.

The most important thing is to find a style that works for you. You are marketing and selling yourself as a unique individual, not some off the shelf product. In my experience, if you want to build personal rapport with people they need to get a sense of the real you. I remember interviewing someone for a job in a bank. He had been a lawyer and answered every question with a perfect, 'text-book' answer. We did not offer him the job as we felt we had not really got to know him as a person. It is not just your ability and experience that gets you a job; personal chemistry and cultural fit count for a lot too. This is especially true as you get higher up within organisations or if you are in a client or customer-facing role.

Steven Covey's book *The 7 Habits of Highly Effective People* contains some fantastic insights and tips for personal effectiveness. The first three Habits centre on feeling self-confident and 'good about yourself'. It is a simple premise that you need to 'sort yourself out' first before you can 'sort others out'. I believe that 'being true to yourself', using a style that works for you, is essential in building rapport and relationships with others. People can sense when you are not being 'genuine' and it tends to make them uncomfortable.

The best example of this was told to me by a friend who worked for Warner Brothers, the media company, during the dotcom boom in the late 1990s. He was constantly being phoned up by Alumni from his business school asking for a networking meeting. After a few meetings he realised that they typically had no interest in developing a relationship with him as a person. They just wanted to be able to 'namedrop' in their next meeting, "of course, when I was talking to Warner Brothers..."; he saw through the insincerity and did not appreciate being 'used'. He would have been a lot more open to helping them, had they spent more time getting to know him as a person and seeing how both parties could help each other out.

By all means learn from successful approaches and styles that other people adopt, but ensure that you adapt these to fit your personality. Jack Welch, former President of General Electric, is widely regarded as a highly successful business leader who achieved great things at GE. He had a unique style that worked for him… just copying his style is unlikely to lead to the same results for others. On a more light-hearted note, I had a boss who could tell really dirty jokes and have all men and women in absolute hysterics. He did it with a twinkle in his eye that meant no one took offence. I imagine that had I (or many others) tried to tell the same jokes, the reaction could have been quite different.

So, in the chapters on Practical Tips (page 58) and Getting Started (page 106), bear this principle in mind. If you really feel uncomfortable going to networking events or using the telephone, make other activities such as one-to-one meetings the focus of your networking efforts. To make the most of networking you will need to attend events and use the telephone. But you can still be a highly effective networker with a small monthly mobile phone bill and only occasional attendance at selected networking events.

3 Effective networkers build long-term relationships based on trust

Trust is a key ingredient to any relationship. Steven Covey in *The 7 Habits of Highly Effective People* writes about the 'Emotional Bank Account' we develop with everyone with whom we have a relationship. This is particularly relevant to the relationships with family and close friends, but can be applied to relationships with new contacts. We are more likely to get help if we are in 'credit'. This takes time to build up, so you need to start somewhere. You might not get much help from a new contact, but you should view networking as developing your relationships over the long-term. Once you have met someone, you can then keep in touch (via email and the occasional meeting) without ever having to work together. After a period of time, you get to the point where your contact will think 'I have known him/her for years', and so are more likely to help.

Think of meeting new contacts as opening that 'Emotional Bank Account' and the subsequent emails, calls and meetings as making small but steady deposits. But remember there is not much point opening a Bank Account if you are not going to make any further deposits! Sowing seeds is another good analogy. Sow enough *and* cultivate them and you get a healthy return on your investment. The difference is that the 'time to harvest' with networking may be long and can be unpredictable. A colleague cited an example of it taking seven years from first meeting a new contact to him winning a piece of business from this contact. But he also added that over those seven years he had always been a useful source of information about the industry, so the relationship had been of some use all along.

Successful, long-term relationships tend to be built on some degree of personal rapport between the two people involved. When you meet new people or are maintaining an old relationship, take the time to build some rapport. This tends to be based on getting to know them as a person outside of work. Do they have a family, what interests them outside of work, where do they go on holiday etc? The beginning and end of meetings, especially if you are walking together to your meeting place (e.g. from reception if going to a meeting room or from their office to the coffee shop and back) are good times to talk more socially.

Make sure you tell them a bit about yourself as well as asking them lots of questions. One former colleague was very happy to pump all of us for information when we were out socialising but he was so tight-lipped about himself that we ended up telling him nothing, because there was no rapport.

An important point to consider when networking with your 'social' friends is to keep business and social life separate. So if you want to tap into their network, rather than do this whilst on a night out, ask for a separate meeting. Try and meet on neutral ground, such as a coffee shop or restaurant, rather than at their or your home and reassure them that you don't want it to get in the way of your friendship, you would just like to get their advice.

4 Know your strengths and play to them; do what you enjoy and are good at

I highly recommend reading a book called *Now, Discover Your Strengths* by Marcus Buckingham and Donald Clifton. Then take their online 'Strengthsfinder' test to find out *your* real strengths. I love the concept of building on your strengths and only addressing your weaknesses if you actually have to use them in your job. It is a lot more fun doing something that you are good at than valiantly battling through something you find difficult. As stated in the book, no matter how hard you work on a weakness, you will never be great at it; working on your strengths is much more likely to lead to better results. Being excellent at a few things will tend to lead to more success than being average to good at lots of things.

Another book you could read is *Brand You – Turn Your Unique Talents into a Winning Formula* by John Purkiss and David Royston-Lee. It has some excellent tools to help you identify your talents, values and purpose and then turn them into a compelling brand that employers, clients and customers will remember.

Gallup, in their Employee Engagement surveys for companies, asks employees to rate their response to the statement: "At work, I have the opportunity to do what I do best every day." It is a great question to ask yourself when considering your next career move.

The first time I lost my job I went to my outplacement consultant and told him all about my strengths and weaknesses. I then concluded I should find a role that helped me improve on my weaknesses. He listened very politely and then in the nicest possible way told me to stop being an idiot. He suggested I find a role that played to my strengths. This would increase my odds of succeeding in that role, thus building on my self-confidence; at that point, I could then start to try and work on some of my weaknesses in a low-risk way.

This seems like an obvious point to make but think about your education and career. Consider how much time you spent with your parents, teachers or managers talking about getting even better at the things you were already good at rather than 'fixing' your weaknesses. Most organisations have a dominant culture and so try and fit employees into that culture; far fewer have the foresight to value diversity and allow each employee to play to their unique strengths. Some people are not great at selling and negotiating, yet there are plenty of people who love the cut and thrust of making a sale or negotiating a deal. Why not let them do it, if it gives them such a kick?

In the Roffey Park survey mentioned in the Introduction, 'being an expert' was highlighted as a key competency for a successful career. A head hunter told me: "It's not just who knows you, but what you are known for. I know a number of people who are well known, but not for doing anything really well." If you are an expert in something *and* people know about you, they (and their networks) will start calling you. As one of my outplacement contacts said: "Keep yourself razor sharp in your field of expertise. That way, you make yourself useful to people." This is linked to **Practical Tip 3** on page 65 – *'Focus on what you want and who you network with'*. Even if you have lost your job you will have some areas of expertise. Be clear on what they are and make sure you keep up to date via informal meetings/calls with your network and published information.

5 Tap into your network's networks

"The only thing worse in the world than being talked about is not being talked about" – Oscar Wilde

A US study in the 1990s (*Getting a Job: A Study in Contacts & Careers*, University Chicago Press 1995) found that 56% had got their jobs through networking. Critically, of this 56%, over 80% got these jobs through what Mark Granovetter called 'weak ties', i.e. a slightly known or recently met contact. The implication of this is that if you can access your network's networks, you can dramatically increase your chances of finding work quickly. So you need to be having many conversations, letting people know what you are looking for. To be able to help you, your contacts need to know that you are looking and the type of role or project work that you are after. This is a variation on the Six Degrees of Separation (the concept that you are never more than six connections away from anyone in the world). This form of networking though only requires two (maybe three) degrees of separation to work for you.

Remember the example in Chapter 1 about how I picked up a very valuable client on the back of a lunch with someone in my network? This was a great case of tapping into someone in my network's network. Given the statistics in Chapter 1 on how jobs are filled, I am convinced that this sort of activity happens for full-time roles as well as consulting projects. In this example I neither knew that the project was available, nor was I known to the people who needed help. What was essential from the perspective of what I did to 'make this happen' was that I had told my network what I was looking for. And the more people that know this, the more likely you are to find people calling you up 'out of the blue'. The other lesson I learnt was the power of the personal recommendation. Had I 'cold-called', I probably would not have got in the door at all, and it certainly would have taken a lot longer to secure any work. If you are using networking to promote your business sales activities, current clients' recommendations can be a very powerful asset. Plan to make the most of them.

Here is another story from someone in my network. A friend of his had been thinking of leaving his role at a consulting firm. He wanted to setup his own business, but lacked the belief he could win sufficient new clients to justify leaving the firm. He casually mentioned his ambitions and insecurity at a dinner party one weekend, and the following Monday received an email headed "This may lead to nothing, but..." It turned out one of the guests at the party was looking for a part-time consultant in the very area this person specialised in; within two months he had left the consulting firm to set up his own business. Two years later he is still acting as a consultant to the new firm. Occasionally, all it takes is letting your friends and close associates know what you're after, and maybe a friend of a friend will be able to help you.

6 It's a two-way thing; give as well as take

"*Give and you shall receive*"

This would appear to be another statement of the obvious, but it is easy to forget, especially when you are in 'need' (as in "I need a job") rather than 'give' mode. Once you view networking as developing long-term relationships with people that are 'give and take', asking for help does not seem like such a bad thing. Even better is to follow **Principle 8** on page 55 – '*Do it while you do not need anything*', and network whilst you are 'in work'. It is just as likely that you may be able to help your contact straight away.

The best example I can give was when I found a new role after several months of looking. Whilst I was in 'need' mode I felt uncomfortable calling people, especially the head hunters, on a regular basis (as all the outplacement and job search advice suggests). Calling once was fine, a second time okay, but then again a month later? Surely they would view me as desperate? (**Principle 2** on page 43 – '*Develop a style that works for you*', suggests you will need to figure out how frequently you feel comfortable calling. As your network expands you are unlikely to have time to contact them too often.) But the moment I had a job, guess what happened? All those head hunters who I had 'needed' suddenly saw me as a potential client. Even the ones that had not returned my calls (see **Practical Tip 11** on page 99 – '*Expect lots of no's, delays, cancellations…it's not personal*') wanted to buy me coffee or even have lunch!

Similarly, I had been talking to consulting firms about doing associate work for them; then, back in full-time employment, I was running some large-scale projects that required consulting support. All of a sudden the boot was on the other foot and many of my contacts came visiting. One consulting firm I freelance for has plenty of examples of employees becoming clients, and clients becoming employees or freelancers. They actively encourage networking, including hosting events for their network of independent consultants, as they see this as a long-term way of growing their business. Other contacts talk about being good at 'connecting people' (Nokia phone not required…), which is part of the 'giving' side of networking. They take time to understand what their networking contacts are looking for (and are good at) and are great at introducing them to people in their own networks that may be able to help.

'Smart' people realise this and so are quite happy to help others when asked. You just never know when one favour gets returned. It is human nature that you are more likely to help someone if they have helped you in the past. So, remember that even if you are in 'need' mode, take the time to find out about what your contact is looking for/interested in as you might be able to help them as well. I have been in a number of such meetings where, because I initiated the meeting and needed help, the introductions have mostly been for my benefit. Nevertheless, I do try and see if there is anything I can do to help the person I am meeting. I certainly feel better about myself if the relationship is two-way, not just me 'taking'. A simple, "You have been really helpful today. If there is any way that I can help you out at all, please do let me know," is all that is needed.

If you have time, make your introductions personally as it sends out a very positive message. Rather than just hand over a contact's email address and telephone number with a 'feel free to use my name', call or send an email yourself. It is also a good example of using **Practical Tip 7** on page 87 – '*Find a reason to call or go and see people*'.

7   Keep high standards

Although one bit of advice I received was "there is no such thing as bad networking", it did continue with "get the quality right and the rest follows". Remember that you are the 'product' being marketed. Think about the image that you want to convey. Develop habits that work for you in terms of returning calls, call when you say you will, follow up meetings with a thank you letter or email, and *always* follow up on actions you said you would do.

If you are out of work, get some good quality, personal business cards made up. They do not cost a lot. It is essential when looking for work that you come across professionally. Even when you are back in work and have a company business card, it can be a nice touch to give someone your personal business card as well. Always have a business card available. You never know when you will bump into someone you'd like to keep in touch with.

Think about how you come across in terms of attitude, body language and dress code. Always be upbeat and positive when 'in public' as this can be infectious. Save your 'down' time for friends, loved ones or being alone. This may be tough if you have been made redundant, but is essential. If you feel awkward about why you left your previous employer, rehearse what you are going to say and don't be too apologetic; it happens so often these days, that it really is nothing to feel bad about. Also, plan to offer this information up fairly early in the conversation (though probably not the first thing you say!). It sounds much better if you tell them by choice rather than in response to the dreaded question "So why did you leave your last company?" If you say it with confidence it is usually not a big deal. If you waffle on, unprepared and lacking confidence, it can really derail the meeting.

Don't be disparaging about others. I am amazed when I hear people, often senior company directors, openly telling me their (negative) opinions of others, sometimes even members of their own departments. It makes me wonder what they say to others about me and lowers my respect for them. Also, we tend to move in quite small circles, so you never know when your 'honest views' may come back to haunt you. You don't have to 'rave' about someone you don't respect, just use a little discretion!

Body language can make a huge difference, and not just when you are in a meeting. Even when you are on the phone, the way you are sitting, facial expressions and voice can all make a huge difference in how you build rapport with your networking contacts (see **Practical Tip 4** on page 72 – 'Communicate by phone').

Dress code is much harder nowadays, given some companies dress down and others are quite formal. If you are not sure, speak to your contact's PA or the switchboard and find out what the dress code is before you meet. Although it is better to err on the more formal side, if you turn up in a suit and your contact is in jeans, this does not help when you are trying to build rapport. And remember that there are some companies that dress smart from Monday to Thursday and then 'dress down' on Fridays.

8 Do it while you do not 'need' anything

The best time to network is when you don't need anything. In
Principle I on page 41, I mention networking contacts not liking
being put under pressure to find you a role. What better way
to meet them than when you really do not need a role? Head
hunters in particular like to find candidates who are already in
good jobs, rather than ones out of work. Remember the adage:
"If you want to get a job done give it to a busy person."

This is easier said than done. You don't need a role because you
already have one; the trouble is that the role you already have
leaves you very little time to network with new and old contacts,
unless directly related to your work. The best advice is "Make
the time!" Try and set aside some time each month, even if only
one hour (that is less than 1% of your working month) to meet
with new contacts or call, email or meet existing contacts. It is
amazing how your existing contacts tend to be too busy to keep
in touch, but if you contact them, they respond and are happy to
speak or meet. My wife says the same thing about calling friends
in the evening. Most of our friends have jobs and young families
and so are fairly worn out in the evening. It is easy to stop calling
old friends as often as we used to, yet when we do they are so
pleased that we made the effort.

Think of it as investing 1% of your working month to increase
your options in the medium to long-term. Your current boss can
get by on 99% of you. If the working day really is too busy, meet
people after work for a drink or send emails in the evening. If you
commute (especially by train and can get a seat) why not write
some update emails or review your database and plan who you

should contact? Even a half hour train journey equates to five hours a week, some of which could be spent on networking.

One idea you could consider is to take the initiative and organise an event. I once organised a reunion of former colleagues who had all left the company we used to work for and gone our separate ways. It started out as quite a small gathering, but as word got round, many more turned up than had originally been planned. Lots of people got back in touch and there was plenty of informal networking. Who knows what it led to, but it was noisy, fun and an easy way for people to catch up. As the organiser, it certainly did my reputation as 'someone who knows everyone' no harm. One of the teams that my wife used to work in organise an annual reunion as the team members have all gone their separate ways now. Many of them work in different companies in the same industry and it can be a really powerful way to network as well as have a lot of fun.

Actively use other opportunities during the year to contact your network by email (see **Practical Tip 4** on page 78 – 'Communicate by email'), such as changing jobs or companies or getting a promotion. How about roping people into sponsoring your charity walk, marathon or skydive? (See **Practical Tip 7** on page 87 – 'Find a reason to call or go and see people'). Try not to leave it all until Christmas, when everybody else is more likely to be doing it.

Summary

- Change your mindset; think of networking as a lifelong way of doing business where you give as well as take. Don't think of it as a) something that you only do when you need a job or help and b) having to go to lots of networking events to benefit from networking... events are just a means to an end, not the end in itself.

- Find ways to network that you feel comfortable doing and be true to yourself. Know your strengths and play to them. Then try out some of the activities that you find harder. But don't make the hard activities the only thing that you do as it is much harder to stick at activities you do not enjoy.

- Don't just think of your own network... think of your network's networks. This will increase the number of people that you can access exponentially.

- Remember to 'give' as well as 'take', even when you are in 'need' mode, i.e. you are asking people for help in finding you a job or project.

- Maintain high standards and a positive outlook at all times when 'in public', even if you are feeling down e.g. because you are out of work.

- Do it when you do not need anything – find some time to network even when you are busy and remember the adage "if you need a job done, give it to a busy person."

Chapter 3:

Putting these principles into practice.
Practical tips for the Reluctant Networker

"Knowing is not enough;

we must apply!"

Johann Wolfgang von Goethe

(German writer)

1 Have a database

At a minimum you will need a database to record information
about your contacts, such as name, organisation, email address and
telephone numbers. I use Microsoft Outlook on my computer
and copy this to my mobile phone, so I have all my contacts stored
in my phone. This is great for keeping in touch with my network
by phone when I have 'dead time', i.e. a spare few minutes in
between meetings, in a taxi or waiting for a plane or train.

Ideally you should segment your database to help you manage
your network most effectively. I have categories such as Clients,
Consultants, each of my former companies, general networking
and one for Acquaintances, i.e. people whose details I want
to keep but with whom I do not actively network. You could
segment by industry type or by priority/importance to you (see
Practical Tip 3 on page 65 – '*Focus*' for how I segment my
marketing campaign). The really organised networkers segment
their contacts list in many different ways… by sector, by role, by
geography, etc.

Try to get some personal information as well, such as partner's
and children's names (even pets!), what sports team they support,
where they went on holiday and add these to the database. They
are great 'ice-breakers' that help you build rapport. If you are
really organised, keep a brief record of when you spoke, emailed
or met them and what you discussed. Apparently Bill Clinton

keeps a card with relevant information on everyone he has met since university.

2   Join a *limited* number of networking websites and networking groups

There are websites such as www.linkedin.com that are *essential* tools in helping you to network. I have signed up to LinkedIn (originated in the USA and with over 60m members worldwide). Although I do not use it as actively as some, I do get regular approaches about jobs and consulting projects and have earned a significant income from these approaches. I was recently invited to a seminar called: "Executive Online Recruitment… Learn how to find your next role online and join a Masterclass on the use of LinkedIn". Head hunters use it as a key way to find people nowadays (one of them described it as 'ridiculously useful'), so if you are looking for a job you really must sign up!

One head hunter told me, "I always look people up on LinkedIn and find it a bit odd if they are not registered. I am amazed at how many CEOs now use LinkedIn." Even if you are a member of social networking websites such as Facebook (and if you are, check the contents of your public profile… are you happy for potential business networking contacts to read all of it?), you should also sign up to a business networking website such as LinkedIn; this is where you will find the people that you are likely to need to network with for business purposes.

Some colleagues have been highly proactive (e.g. using the Industry or Special Interest Groups) and have found it an essential tool for their networking activities. For example, one person used it to find industry 'experts' for a new supply chain project he had been assigned and for which he had only limited experience. Other sites are Viadeo (originated in France and with 25m members), Xing (originated in Germany with roughly 8m members) and Naymz (originated in the USA with over 1m members). Some are free for basic use and charge for premium services, others charge for basic membership. It takes only a few minutes to register. Make sure your profile includes 'key words' people would use to find you, e.g. the industry sectors you work in and the roles you have done/would like to do.

But signing up to a number of online networking websites does not replace the need to network face-to-face. Think of the websites as enabling the *quantity* of your networking. They are a great way to communicate with millions of people in a low-cost, time-effective way. But the *quality* of this networking is limited, especially with new contacts where you have yet to build rapport. This is where face-to-face networking comes in.

There are numerous networking groups that you can join. For example, there are ones for entrepreneurs, lawyers, women, senior international executives. Some are local, others international. BNI (Business Network International www.bni.com) has over 5,000 local groups in over 40 countries meeting weekly. According to their website their membership of over 100,000 passed on more than 5.5 million referrals that generated €1.65bn worth of business!

These groups tend to meet on a regular basis and allow members to network with each other for all sorts of different reasons. You may have to pay a subscription fee to join, so do your research beforehand to see if the group you want to join really will help. For example, you could talk to some existing members to find out how it has helped them and to see if their way of networking is one that suits you. Some groups are quite relaxed and informal, others more aggressive in how members help each other out (and expect to be helped). The group of which I am a member has a lot of independent consultants and regularly 'broadcasts' consulting opportunities for its members and their networks. Some assignments have been staffed entirely with members of this network. There are also (often daily) broadcasts about new jobs, many of which have not been advertised.

I also attend networking evenings of the two groups from my Business School that fit my profile. At one of these events I met a number of interesting people but left thinking that none of the conversations were likely to lead to anything. To my surprise a few months later I got an email from someone I had met that evening. I subsequently joined a colleague of hers on a long-term consulting assignment. So, on the one hand it is hard to know which conversations will lead to anything, but on the other hand, you can increase your chances of success by targeting the right events to attend.

My advice is to try a number of these different networking organisations and to read **Practical Tip 8** on page 88 – 'Networking events'. Find out how they can help you given how you like to interact with people and how much time you want to invest in networking. But be focused on the ones that really can help you. As a Reluctant Networker you are unlikely to love spending your evenings/breakfasts at networking events, so make sure that when you do go it is likely to lead to something. That includes picking the networking groups that are most likely to be of use for your own needs. You can spend huge amounts of time both online and at events that will not deliver much in terms of output.

In summary, don't believe the people who tell you that online sites are replacing face-to-face networking, nor those that say the opposite, i.e. you cannot replace the face to face aspect of networking so signing up to LinkedIn is unnecessary. The reality is that you need to do both!

3 Focus on *what* you want and *who* you network with

Focus on *what* you want: your target sector, role or project

Without focus, networking could become a never-ending exercise that is more than a full-time job.

Think about this excerpt from Lewis Carroll's *Alice's Adventures in Wonderland*:

"'Would you tell me, please, which way I ought to go from here?'
'That depends a good deal on where you want to get to,' said the Cat.

'I don't much care where –' said Alice.

'Then it doesn't matter which way you go,' said the Cat.'"

So, unlike Alice, you can help yourself by narrowing down the list of potential networking contacts. There are many ways to do this.

You need to be clear on the type of role or organisation you are looking for. Having a very specific target sector and role has two benefits. Firstly, it allows you to focus your time and efforts, which should increase your odds of success. If you write down all your contacts and then think about your contacts' contacts, you could go and meet with a lot of people. This might be fun if you are into meeting people, but you could find yourself a 'busy fool'. Lots of contacts will have a meeting with you, but will it lead to anything productive? Meetings take up a lot of time and you will need to judge when you want to 'invest' time in developing a lead. This is quite a tough one to call.

To help me focus, I have a one page list of 'What success looks like' over the next one to two years. This is a list of things I want to have achieved and with realistic timescales. It is written as a series of statements of what I will have achieved at the end of it. For example one could be "Have set up my own consulting business"; another could be "Have written a book on networking". Some people have a very specific long-term career plan (e.g. I want to be a Director of a medium/large company in 10 years). Like the many people I know, I have struggled to say with conviction where I really want to be in 10 years. Even if I did I would not know how to get there. 'What success looks like' is a great way to help me manage my time and ensure I'm going in the right direction.

The second benefit of having a clear role/sector focus, is that it makes it easier for people to help you. Make it easy for them, so they have to do as little thinking and doing as possible. Offer to do the follow up for them, so long as they give you the contact details and say it is okay to use their name when you make contact. **Practical Tip 11** on page 99 – 'Expect lots of no's' talks about how busy people are and where helping you fits in their list of priorities. If it is just a case of looking up a few contact details in their contacts database, you will be more likely to get the introductions you want. Another side benefit is keeping control.

I had an excellent meeting once when a new contact not only offered to introduce me to several great contacts of his but also said he would write to them himself. Although this was incredibly kind, to some degree it backfired on me, because I was not in control of my own marketing. Most of the introductions were great but at the last minute he added another name that we had not discussed fully. It was to a person I had met a couple of years before, so I came across as rather unprofessional to that contact. Now I always offer to do the 'contacting' work myself and keep control of my own marketing.

Once you are clear on your areas of focus, develop your own version of the '30 second elevator pitch', except make it *shorter*. What are the top two or three things you want people to remember you for? Although I do consulting on a much wider range of projects and sectors, if someone asks me what I do or needs a one liner for a biography for a networking event, I say: "I'm a consultant that specialises in strategy, category management and M&A in the retail sector." That is about as much as I can hope people will remember when they come across relevant projects in the months or years after we meet. So make sure you are very clear about which functional roles or projects you want to take on and in which industry sectors you want to operate in.

Focus on *who* you network with

The other way to focus is to be clear on who you network with. The best way to think about this is on two levels: what sort of help can this person provide and how likely are they to help? Good people with whom to network typically fit into one or more of the following criteria:

- ◆ Decision-makers.
- ◆ Good networkers.
- ◆ Business friends.
- ◆ Former colleagues.

If you can find people who meet all four criteria, hang on to them as they will be great networking allies for you!

Decision-makers – Networking with decision-makers sounds like a pretty obvious thing to do. The trick is to find out who the decision-makers are. In general, the higher up an organisation an individual is, the greater influence he or she will have over decisions. The key issue is whether they will decide on the specific role or project that you want to secure.

For example, I had a meeting with a chief executive about some consulting work within his organisation. He was happy to identify business units in his company where I might be able to help. He was also happy to introduce me to the heads of these business units. However, he was clear that he would not tell them to use me. If they had a need and asked him for his advice he would recommend me, but it was up to them to make the decision. When I contacted one of the business unit heads, he passed me onto the relevant country manager that might need the help, again saying that using my consulting services would be up to the country manager.

What are the lessons from this? Firstly, it pays to ask the question early on: "Who will be making the final decision on this?" Secondly, you should not assume that the people highest up in the organisation will make the decision. Nevertheless, they may be able to get you a meeting with the person that does make the decision. The third lesson is that even if there is only one actual decision-maker, there will probably be other people influencing the decision. For example if a manager is recruiting someone, he or she will probably have the final say, but his or her boss as well as members of the team may well have an input into the decision. The more you can understand how a decision will be taken the more likely you are to be able to influence it. It all sounds like obvious advice, but it can easily be forgotten when you are pitching for a role or some work.

Good networkers – Although there may be more than you might think, not everyone is a Reluctant Networker! Some people are natural networkers and so have a wide and active network that they are happy to use for your benefit. But even Reluctant Networkers can be good networkers if they have seen the value of it and developed a style that works for them (see Chapter 2 on page 38 – 'Networking Principles'). As I build my own network, I find I am able to help people more and more.

Senior members of the business community, including people who are now retired, are often good networkers for two reasons. Firstly, they will have built up a wide network during their business careers. Secondly, they will probably have seen how networking helped them and so are more likely to want to help others, especially people at an earlier stage of their careers, in need of advice and some introductions.

If you are fortunate enough to have (or have had) a mentor either inside or outside your current company, don't just think of them as someone to turn to for advice on what to do. They too, will probably have a good network and so can make some useful introductions for you.

You can find out pretty quickly if a contact is a good networker or not. Do they offer up suitable new leads and contacts when you ask for advice? Do you ever get calls from new contacts saying that 'xyz' had given them your name? These are both signs of a good networker.

Business friends – The people who are most likely to help are your 'business friends'; this does not mean your friends from work who you go out to lunch with or for drinks after work; these people will help you but may not have the best contacts in other organisations to help you get the role or assignment you are looking for. Business friends are people who know you in a business context and are willing to recommend you – you do not need to be friends in the social sense.

Think of it this way. If a head hunter or recruitment agency called this contact to ask for a reference on you for a job, would they give you a (genuinely) positive recommendation? If the answer is yes, they are probably a business friend. Typically, business friends are also former colleagues (see below) but you may have some with whom you have not worked in the past. For example, you may have school or university friends who can help you. Or you may have been a client, customer or supplier and worked closely with someone who would recommend you. You may also have known a head hunter for many years that would be willing to help.

Why are business friends so important? Over the course of my career it has become clear to me that personal chemistry is the key, not only to developing strong relationships but also to being successful in a role. I have seen this happen to others many times and even experienced it myself. How often have you witnessed a new boss arriving and changing several members of his or her team? When this happened how often was it due to a lack of ability to do the role and how often a lack of ability to do the role *the way the boss wanted it done*? I had been in a role for a while when a new boss arrived. His perception of me was completely different to that of his predecessor. The first one had rated me, the other did not, yet I had not changed either my style or what I was doing. Obviously you are more likely to get help from a former boss that rates you, i.e. your business friend.

The other benefit of networking with 'business friends' is that it is more fun, so you are more likely to do it. Forcing yourself to call up and try and meet with people you really don't respect or like is not much fun. In addition you are less likely to come across as sincere and genuine in your reasons for meeting.

Former colleagues – For Reluctant Networkers former colleagues can be a really powerful source of contacts and information. One thing that puts Reluctant Networkers off networking is having to contact new people. At least with former colleagues you don't have to worry about not knowing them. If you think you cannot contact them because it has been so long since you last spoke, please read **Practical Tip 6** on page 83 – '*It's never too late to get back in touch*'. Not speaking to someone for a few years is not a good enough reason to avoid calling!

Think about all the people that you have worked with in the past and where they are now working, let alone the other organisations that they worked in during their careers. Use your membership of www.linkedin.com to reconnect with former colleagues and university classmates. This is a huge network that is relatively easy to access and you do not have to use the dreaded cold call method. Remember the example in Chapter 2 about a former colleague who built his consulting activities largely around his network of our former colleagues? This network of former colleagues has huge potential if you choose to put it to good use. So long as you give as well as take (see **Principle 6** on page 51) it is not about 'using' people, a common justification Reluctant Networkers give for not networking more actively.

In summary, try and focus on people who meet as many of the above criteria as possible. The former boss that I mentioned in Chapter 2 who made introductions to new clients for me meets all four criteria. You probably will not have many that meet all four, but even if they meet two criteria, it is likely to be a useful contact for networking.

I segment my consultancy marketing campaign into an 'A' List: 'Friends with budgets', 'B' List: 'Friends who may have a budget or can introduce me to the people with the budgets' and 'C' List: 'Friends but who probably can't help much or people I am not sure are business friends'. You can waste a lot of time contacting 'non-friends' who will rarely *tell* you they won't help. They just tend to not return your calls or postpone your meetings.

4 Communicate, using all media

It goes without saying that communication is an essential part of networking. There is no point having a great database of contacts or being a member of networking sites and organisations if you are not going to communicate with the members of your network. But remember that communication can be done by a number of different media. The most obvious ones are verbal (telephone), written (email and letters) and face-to-face (meetings and attending events). This tip focuses on the phone, email and face-to-face meetings. Events are covered in **Practical Tip 8** on page 88. It starts with the phone, a tool that is usually underutilised by Reluctant Networkers!

Communicate by phone

"I am always doing things I can't do – that's how I get to do them" – Pablo Picasso

Some people love talking on the telephone, others are less comfortable. Personally I find the phone quite a difficult means of communicating with people I do not know very well. Judging by an informal survey of friends and colleagues, Reluctant Networkers tend to find the telephone a difficult communication tool. This is especially true when they need to use it for what they perceive as 'difficult' situations, e.g. cold calling new contacts, getting back in touch with former colleagues or trying to sell or market something. For example, when I was at university I had to raise money from companies to support a student society. I used to dread the phone calls, breaking out into a cold sweat when I actually had to ask for the money. In these 'difficult' situations I am much more comfortable writing letters and then following this up with a face-to-face meeting, where I can see the other person's body language and build more rapport.

My natural instinct when I need to get in touch with someone is to email rather than to use the phone. After several years of networking, however, I do recommend that in general, calling someone is better than emailing them. It is a better way to build rapport as you can start with some social chit chat. And you generally find out more from a two-way, 'real time' phone call than a one-way email that may or may not get a response. If you don't get through you can always send a follow-up email saying that you called and explaining why.

A good example of why using the telephone is better comes from many years back before I became a more 'seasoned' networker. Although it is not an example from networking, it was a useful lesson in the value of the telephone as a two-way means of communication. Whilst looking for a job, I made the mistake of trying to negotiate the final stages of an offer by letter and email. I had had a couple of face-to-face meetings and we had reached the 'final offer' stage. The company was located some 200 miles away from my home so I did not want to go back again in person. The company's 'final' offer was still a little way off what I was expecting. I convinced myself that a letter was the best way to respond as there were many points to cover and a letter left no room for misunderstanding. Although this was true I am sure that my dislike of the telephone for these types of situation also influenced my decision to write. However, by responding by letter I missed the opportunity to engage in a two-way conversation. The company responded to my letter with an emailed letter and discussions ended without us reaching agreement. I never did find out if we could have bridged the gap in our positions. A telephone conversation would have been much more likely to achieve this. With hindsight a telephone call, followed up with a letter confirming what had been agreed and any outstanding issues would have been more productive.

Here is another, more recent, example. A client had not responded to a number of phone calls and was well past the due date for paying my bill. I was half-way through typing an irate email, when I decided that a phone call would be better. He had been ill, chased up the bill immediately and gave me a contract extension!

Putting these principles into practice

An outplacement contact whose clients can work in his company's office whilst they look for a job told me, "It's always the ones on the phone who get the jobs quicker than the ones working at the computer." His advice for job seekers was to call at least one person in your network every day.

On a practical note, emails do not always reach their intended target. One of my contacts responded several weeks after I had sent out an email, apologising that he had only just found my email. It had been filtered out into his 'junk email' folder even though we had exchanged emails extensively a few months earlier when I had been doing a project for his business.

So, if you already use the phone all the time, keep doing it! For those people who are not naturals on the phone, my advice is to make yourself use it more! If you can manage to change your mindset it will be a lot easier. This is linked to the networking principle 'It's all in the mind'. Start by making the mental leap that the phone is a vital networking tool that can help you achieve your goals. You probably already know this but have convinced yourself that it is not really for you. Once you have made this leap, start practising. The more you do it, the easier it will become.

Remember what it was like not being able to ride a bicycle and how practice overcame those initial fears? And to continue the analogy, you do not need to be a serious road racer, mountain biker or even be able to cycle 'hands-free' to be able to benefit from cycling. It is the same with networking. You will probably never come to love using your phone and it may take some practice, but any increase in its usage is likely to be to your benefit. One of my outplacement contacts' top tips was "Overcome your fear by developing a habit… and taking action develops a habit."

Try not to let yourself be put off by the occasional 'difficult' call that did not quite go according to plan. This may be 'easier said than done', but you really will need to use the phone if you want to network successfully. The quicker you develop a phone style that works for you the better.

Here are a few practical suggestions, mainly aimed at people who are using networking to find a new role:

♦ Tell them you are going to ring in advance: Try to send an email in advance of calling so that the other person knows that you are going to call, *when* you are going to call and *what* the call will be about. This is polite and also gives the other person time to think how they can help. It also makes the call easier when you come to make it as you have committed to call them and they are expecting your call.

♦ Block out the time and do several at a time: If you are making difficult calls, say to people whom you haven't seen for a while, plan time in your diary on a regular basis and then try and do several at the same time. You get into the swing and it becomes much easier. The first call is always the hardest one, so find something to motivate you… I was told about someone who used to kick a ball around in the garden with his son to get his adrenalin going. Even if you have a particularly good or bad call, keep going through the list of who you said you would call during that phone session. If your contact is not there, leave a message that you called with your number but say that you will call back. Don't rely on people returning your calls (see **Practical Tip 11** on page 99 – '*Expect lots of no's, delays…*')

- Just do it! Don't wait until you have all your ducks in a row before you start calling… there is no substitute for just calling; if there is a job going and you have the right skills, a poor phone technique is not going to stop you getting the job… not calling at all is! Remember that, so long as you are polite and professional, most people really are quite happy to listen and to try and help.

- Give them something too: Think in advance if there is anything that you can do to help them (e.g. contacts or industry insights). Then once you have talked through how they can help you say something like: "I really appreciate all your help… if there is anything I can do to help you, please let me know"; often, just the offer of help is enough.

- Make notes before, during and after: Jot down the points you want to raise during the conversation so you don't forget any key things you want to ask; you may find it helpful to write out your opening few sentences and rehearse them before you call; take notes during the call especially of any follow-up contact names, numbers and email addresses; after the call write up a brief note of what came out of it.

- Ask if you can call again: It is always easier to ask the other person if they would mind if you called again, than sitting there a week later thinking 'I can't bother that person again so soon'. Usually, people will say "of course, I'd like to hear how you are getting on anyway."

- Ask for any other contacts: Ask the other person if they could suggest one or two other people whom you could approach using the other person's name as an introduction.

- Say 'thank you': Send an email to thank the other person for their help after the call.

- Smile! One successful salesman I know has a laminated picture of a 'smiley face' on his desk for when he made his calls. He was convinced that smiling whilst talking on the phone made a positive difference.

- Posture: Some people stand up, look out of the window and use a headset when making calls. This avoids them being hunched up at their desk, which is not ideal for projecting a self-confident, positive image.

Remember that you need to develop a style that works for you, so you may not find all of the above suggestions helpful... pick the ones that help you to spend more time on the phone. See Chapter 4 on page 106 for more suggestions on how to get started.

Communicate by email: it is a great, quick way to keep in touch

"I really hate networking, having to call people up all the time on the telephone... thank god for email." This is a quote from a contact of mine who is a director of a well-known, major UK company. Email is a great tool for all sorts of networkers, especially Reluctant Networkers.

Despite the above point recommending the phone over email, email is a great networking tool as well. Remember when written communication had to be done by post or fax? Email is a wonderful tool for easily staying in touch with your network, is so quick and costs nothing. As you build your network it is increasingly time-consuming to keep in touch by telephone on a regular basis. Email can plug that gap.

If nothing else, plan a bit of time in December to send out a Christmas eCard and update your network. Unless you have a strong relationship with someone because you have known them for years or worked together, you will need to keep your network 'live' so that people remember you. Remember making deposits into Steven Covey's Emotional Bank Account in **Principle 3** on page 45? Just because you met someone once does not mean that they will think of you when they come across the perfect opportunity for you. Christmas email is a great excuse to get back in touch with people and can be a good excuse to suggest meeting, even if only to 'catch up'. I always end up with a load of meetings, drinks, lunches or dinners in January and February as a result of Christmas emails.

Use the 'blind copy' facility if you are OK with sending a standard email, as then the recipients do not see who else and how many people have been sent the same email. This is most relevant for short updates such as a new address/contact details. If you prefer something more personal, but also quick, have a 'standard' couple of paragraphs that you 'cut and paste' and personalise the start and end. My only word of caution is that when I did this a few years ago, my internet provider threw me out and threatened to close my account as they thought I was sending spam! Make sure that you regularly check your junk email folder for emails that have been sent to you.

Communicate why you are communicating

Some people in your network will be used to periodic phone calls from members of their network just to 'catch up'. They may also be used to people calling them up and asking for advice on their job search. Others may not be used to it, especially from you if you are doing it for the first time. I came across an (admittedly extreme) case of a networking catch up call done by a former colleague who was greeted with a frosty, "Why are you *really* calling me, what do you want?"

So it is worth being prepared to explain why you are getting in touch. If you are emailing or writing it is pretty standard to explain the purpose of your contact. If you are phoning and need their help for job search try and get this into the conversation fairly early on after some initial ice-breakers. But even if you have no specific reason for calling, from my experience it is fine to say, "I'm just calling to catch up on how you are getting on as we have not spoken for a while." I usually use the telephone to set up a face-to-face meeting as this is how I prefer to network. However, as my network has expanded, and given time pressures, quite a few of my telephone calls end up in lengthy 'catch up' style conversations.

Spend more time in coffee shops

Remember that being an *effective* networker does not necessarily mean that you have to attend lots of networking events. The key thing is that you are spending time broadening and deepening your network by meeting old and new contacts. *How* you do this can be adapted to your own style. Realising this was a bit of a 'light-bulb' moment for me, as I then realised that networking could be good fun.

Putting these principles into practice

If I analysed where I spend the majority of my time on networking it is likely to be in coffee shops. As a Reluctant Networker I am much more comfortable meeting people in my network a) in person and b) on a one to one basis. I prefer to have fewer, more meaningful networking relationships, where I can really get to know someone and build a good rapport. Coffee shops offer a much more informal environment than going to meet someone at their office (and not everyone has an 'office' these days anyway), where you may feel that it is more of a business meeting than an informal networking catch up. Coffee shops are the new mobile offices… have a look when you next go into one during the week and see how many people are having informal business meetings.

5 If you 'want' something from your networking, be prepared and make it easy for people to help you

Here are a couple of lessons from another real example: be prepared to move fast and do your homework before meetings. A friend had been introduced to the chairman of a business and had been in email contact with him for a few months. Suddenly the chairman called one evening and asked to meet him two days later. Then he handed the phone over to someone else whose opening words were "I'm xxx, please send me your CV to (email address)". This friend was caught short on many fronts: he had not been expecting such short notice and so had to cancel some other meetings to fit it in; he did not have a pen on him to write down the email address and did not have a clue who the second person was as it was all so quick. He then did not do much research on the company (as he was too busy the previous evening) or on the location which turned out to be a casino. He went dressed in casual attire and everyone in the club had a jacket and tie. The chairman even commented on his clothes. It was also obvious that he had not researched the web site (the second person was CEO) – which did not start things off well, all due to being caught off guard. Amazingly, he secured an interim role in the company six months later!

Here is another real example from one of my contacts on how good preparation can help you secure a role: He helped a good friend get a job by achieving a great impression with the chairman in his interview. He helped him build a very detailed financial picture of the company's performance with a detailed presentation that showed in the interview:

- Five year financial performance of the company.
- 'View' about market growth and market share over this period.
- A detailed financial comparison of the nearest competitor to the company.
- Completed 'in store' study of merchandising, packaging, pricing, and range architecture versus the major competitor.
- Recommendations for (a) organic growth (b) profit growth.

In the middle of the presentation, the chairman got up and congratulated him on what was the best business overview of one of his companies he had ever seen!

This is a great example of how you can use the people in your network to improve your understanding of industries or companies that interest you. Also if you have access to databases (e.g. outplacement agencies often offer this for their candidates), make the most of them. Similarly, you should make sure you can access trade journals and newspapers for your chosen industries.

Websites and Google searches are an amazing source of information. When I was looking for a publishing agent for this book, I was given an introduction by an old friend. I looked the agent up on Google and found his website. There I saw that he was also the agent for another contact of mine. So I called my other contact up and, as a result, got a second introduction to the agent. I am sure that the combination of two introductions from trusted sources helped me build professional rapport with him before we had even met.

6 It is never too late to get back in touch

"Better late than never"

It *really* is never too late to get in touch with old contacts. Of course it is better to have maintained the relationship over the years, but better late than never. I have heard friends try and convince themselves that "it has been too many years" or "they might not remember me" or "why would they want to hear from me after all these years?" Remember the principle of "It's all in the mind." So why not turn the question on its head and ask: "Why would they *not* want to hear from me?" It is amazing how pleased former colleagues almost always are to hear from you again. I got back in touch with someone I had met on an aeroplane some four years earlier. I sent an email entitled "We met on a plane a few years ago...", contact was re-established and we now actively help each other out in business. It turned out he lives next door to one of my wife's university friends and we have much else in common. I have written and published a business school case study together with a contact of one of his contacts, six years after getting back in touch and ten years after our initial meeting.

If you are calling because you are looking for work, most will be flattered that you thought of them in seeking help or career advice. Call them up and say something along the lines of "I'm considering options and thought of you as someone who can give advice and maybe bounce a few ideas off; you also know a few people and I'd welcome any suggestions of others you think I should meet; can I buy you a coffee some time?" Use some flattery if needed, such as "a number of people have told me how well you are doing and suggested that I speak to you." So many people I speak to say this type of approach can lead to people offering several really relevant introductions. In fact, 'needing' something can be a good reason to get back in touch in the first place. Just remember that once you have re-established contact you should then keep in touch on a more regular basis.

Here is a real example of how one friend got a new role: he was reading a newspaper one day and saw an article mention his (soon to be) new boss. They had met nine years before when the boss had offered him a job that he had had to turn down. Irrespective of the fact that my friend had not kept in touch with him for nine years, he wrote to him. He asked if he remembered him, told him what he'd been up to, that he was looking for new challenges and asked if he could help him out in any way. He replied back within a week saying it was good to hear from him and that he'd keep an eye out. Four months later he called out of the blue with a new opportunity which my friend accepted. As my friend said: "This is not to blow my own trumpet, but to point out that you must never be put off contacting someone you haven't seen or spoken to for several years, especially if you got on well with them."

Even if you did *not* get on well, it may be worth getting back in touch if you think someone may be able to help. Here is another example from someone in my network:

He had had a very negative relationship with a member of his team that he had 'inherited' when he joined the company. The team member had wanted his job and so resented reporting to him. They did not hit it off and so the team member left about twelve months later. Nine years later, my contact had been made redundant and was starting to network to find a new role. He had no plans to get back in touch with this former colleague, given the bad terms on which they had left all those years before. However, in a short space of time, three of his networking contacts suggested this person as someone with whom he should talk to develop his contacts.

So my contact plucked up courage and rang him. After maybe a difficult minute or so, things started to 'warm up'. He started by congratulating him on his career success to date (flattery really can get you a long way), and asked him to give a quick update on the challenges he had faced to date. He also knew the person's boss well, and dropped into the conversation the great feedback that the boss had given about him. He then asked if the person would mind giving him some help.

The result was amazing. As my contact says: "I cannot tell you how much help and support I have received, in little over a month: detailed industry contacts list, useful head-hunter contacts and even several hours' work of key industry information prepared for me, to aid in future interviews. The lesson for me was to be brave, break down the barriers, recognise the strengths people have and show a little humility."

So it can be worthwhile making a point to 'bury the hatchet'. As another example, one of my networking contacts was made redundant by his boss, who was then himself made redundant a few months later. Rather than gloat, he picked up the phone to him and they met for lunch as he recognised him as a useful networking contact. They had fallen out professionally, not personally – there is a big difference. They now meet for lunch regularly and the former boss has passed on a number of networking contacts.

Please note that this does not contradict **Practical Tip 3** on page 65 – *'Focus on who you network with'*. Just make sure that you have a good reason for getting back in touch with the former boss or colleague who had not been a 'business friend' when you last worked together. The example above of three people recommending contacting the same former colleague would count as a good reason!

One simple thing to do is to use www.linkedin.com (see **Practical Tip 2** on page 62). When you register make sure you list all the companies for which you have worked as well as all the universities and colleges you have attended. Then you can do an easy 'search' for former colleagues and classmates. LinkedIn will show you everyone else registered with them that has worked/studied at the places you have been at. You can select the people you know and LinkedIn sends them an 'invitation to connect'. When your former colleagues/ classmates accept the invitation you are notified. However, don't just leave it at that... it is then really easy to send them an email and re-establish the contact. Try and arrange to meet or at least call them (if they are now based in a different location). If you have worked for a large organisation LinkedIn may have a 'Group' of current and former employees of that organisation that you can easily join.

7 Find a reason to keep in touch, call or go and see people

If you are going to network with people on a regular basis, rather than just when you 'need' something, you will need to have some reasons for contacting people. Sometimes, it can be as simple as a call saying, "We have not spoken for a while; it would be great if we could meet for a coffee or drink to catch up." Once you have met it is then much easier to call once in a while to stay in touch.

There are other things you can use as a reason to contact people. Some are a result of new things you have done recently or are about to do such as a new job, new project, an article you have written or a charitable event you are organising. Another tip is a bit more 'tactical'. I have got to see many (often senior executives) people that I did not know that well, purely by contacting them to say, "I'm in the area on a particular date, have you got a spare 30 minutes that day?" On one occasion I had arranged a meeting with a friend in one company and then 'used' that meeting as an excuse to contact the more senior executives with an "I'm in the building anyway, do you have some time then?" One was available that day and even though the other one was out of the office then, it led to a meeting a few weeks later.

The other easy way to do this is to 'help' someone else by introducing them to other people in your network that you want to keep in touch with. An email or call saying you would like to introduce someone else is a perfect excuse to get in touch. Another idea is to forward interesting articles on to people in your network. With the internet it is so easy to copy the hyperlink and email with a 'thought you might be interested in the attached' message. If I come across jobs or projects that could be of interest to people in my network I am happy to take a minute or two to forward on to them. All these activities are consistent with **Principle 6** on page 51 – *'It's a two-way thing; give as well as take'*.

8 If you are going to go to networking events, make the most of them

Reluctant Networkers tend not to enjoy networking events. I'm not a natural when it comes to 'working a room' full of strangers at a networking event. I prefer to network in smaller groups or even better one on one. I am pretty sure that many other people find these events quite daunting, especially the first few that they go to. Nevertheless, networking events can be an invaluable source of new contacts and information. I won a significant piece of business as a result of meeting someone at such an event. A few months later her colleague called me as she had a project that needed my skills. The lead only came about from my attendance at that event. So I do go to a selected few that I think may be able to help me. Here is some advice, based on my experience and with the overall rule, 'if you are going to go, make the most of them':

- Be selective. Focus on events that are likely to have people that you will want to network with in the future; if you start going to events and they don't lead to anything useful you are likely to be put off, given that it is unlikely to be an activity that you naturally enjoy: also go to ones where you are likely to meet the same people, so that you can start to build a relationship with people that you meet more than once.

- Be clear why you are going. Even though I now enjoy many of the ones I go to, I would not choose to go to them in my 'free time'. I need to get something productive out of them such as some new contacts or old contacts revived. I have also got some great tips on books I have subsequently read. Saying hello to most of the room without really 'connecting' does not achieve my objectives (save that for the celebrities…). I prefer to have several conversations that are long enough to 'make a connection' (i.e. do we get on/want to keep in touch going forward and so we should exchange business cards), but not so long that I only have one or two.

- If you go with a friend, split up and meet people you don't know. By all means introduce each other to interesting people you have met and leave together but remember this is a networking event, not a drink with a friend.

- For similar reasons, if you meet friends you see regularly, say hello, but, again, go off and meet new people.

- If there is a delegate list, see if there is anyone you particularly want to see (old contacts, people who work at companies or in industries you are interested in) and go and find them; your hosts can always help with introductions, so a "I'd really like to meet xyz, would you mind introducing me?" should do the trick; I know people who get the guest list in advance of the event, so they can prepare not only who they want to see but also what they want to say to them.

- Be confident! Make eye contact regularly, smile and look like you are a natural. There will be many others in the room not feeling 100% confident and in their element… it is not just you who will be feeling like that. If you look like you would rather be somewhere else, you are unlikely to meet many people and have useful conversations. I used to joke with a friend that when I went to big parties at university I used to 'flick on my sociable switch'. I made a real effort to come across as very sociable and, as a result, had a reputation as 'somebody who knew everybody'. When my (now) wife met me at university, even she says I was perceived to be a natural networker... appearances can be deceptive! The reality was that I found those parties quite hard work but 'flicking the switch' helped me change my mindset and ensure I made the most of them.

♦ When you turn up, you'll probably need to start a conversation. If you are not that skilled at these events, it may be easier to talk to someone else on their own. It can be harder to break into an existing group, unless you know someone in the group already. Have a few questions ready to get the conversation going along the lines of "Hello, I'm xyz, do you know many people here?", "Where have you come from?", "What line of work are you in?" "What brings you to this event?" Be prepared to talk about yourself as well and share information. You do not just have to ask the questions. Once you are more confident, you can 'barge in' on established groups in a polite way. Make sure you listen as well as talk; people love to talk about themselves, so don't just ask some questions (with sincerity!) but practice 'active listening', it's a great way to build rapport.

♦ If you are already in a group talking, keep an eye out for people trying to join you. Turn your body to 'let them in' and in a break in the conversation, tell them what is being discussed and introduce yourself; this is a nice gesture that will be much appreciated, especially by others who are not natural 'event networkers'.

♦ Moving on to another conversation can also be difficult. But remember that this is a networking event, so it is OK to have lots of short conversations, rather than one long one. If you are in a group, you can excuse yourself, saying something like,

"Will you excuse me, but I need to go and catch up with xyz over there/I need to find xyz as I am keen to talk to him/her." You can do this even if you know no-one else. It is harder if you are only with one other person, but you can still say the same things to 'extricate' yourself from a conversation that has gone on too long. If you have met some other people already, why not introduce the person you are talking to now to them? "Will you excuse me/it's been a pleasure talking to you, but I need to go and catch up with xyz over there. Before I do, can I introduce you to some other people I have met?" These tend to be more effective (and less embarrassing) than the "I need a drink or I need to go to the toilet" ways of getting out of conversations I used to use at parties when I was younger.

♦ One friend has what he calls "The Five Question rule." If after asking a new contact five questions they have still not asked him any questions it's time to move on! These sorts of people tend not to be very helpful.

♦ If you take somebody's business card and you enjoyed meeting them, jot down on the back of the card some memorable details from your conversation, e.g. what work they do. Then enter their contact details in your database and drop them an email the next day saying you enjoyed meeting and hope you can stay in touch. This makes it easier to get back in touch months or even years later, when you do want to ask their advice. If it is so long ago that you think they may not remember you, try "We met at xyz networking event last year" in the title of your email or if you have to leave a voicemail… it works almost every time (see **Practical Tip 6** on page 83 – 'It is never too late to get back in touch'). The memorable details you wrote down on the back of the card will help give you an ice-breaker when you get back in touch – "So are you still doing xyz job?"

- If they don't have any cards (it is amazing how many people don't have any or enough at these events), ask them to write their name, telephone number and email address down on the back of a spare one of yours.
- Set yourself a goal of *speaking* at an event that fits your profile once in a while. This may sound ambitious for a Reluctant Networker but when you think about it, what better way to raise your profile and have lots of people coming to talk to you after your talk? It is not as difficult as you might think. The organisers of these events are always on the lookout for speakers. The key is to talk about something on which you are an expert and an enthusiast. Even if you do not like public speaking, giving a talk on something you know and are passionate about is quite easy and your passion and expertise will come across. It also helps to 'self-select' the people you speak to afterwards as they know something about you and have chosen to come and talk to you, so you may well have something in common.

9 You'll need to network with both men and women

One of my outplacement contacts has worked with a number of female clients who have found it awkward to network with men. They are concerned about how their approaches may be interpreted. As a result they often end up doing most of their networking with other women. His advice is that women need to network with men, because a purely female network base is likely to be too restricting. Some of his female clients even say that other successful women can be a woman's worst enemy and that men are often so much more helpful. There is immense scope for women to network with men if they can just find a style that makes them feel comfortable.

This can also be an issue for men; some may feel awkward networking with women, either out of shyness or old fashioned views about women in the workplace. It has to be better to choose your network based on the four criteria on page 68 (e.g. business friends, former colleagues), rather than gender. The really effective networkers that I know (both male and female) have a wide network of women and men.

Given my gender I carried out an informal survey of women in my network to get their perspective on:

(a)   Is networking for women different than for men?

(b)   What approaches can you adopt if you think that networking with the opposite sex could be awkward?

(c)   What approaches work best for you?

Two things struck me about their comments. One was that (apart from a few awkward instances) gender is not really the issue. So if it is for you, you may need to apply **Principle 1** to this, i.e. '*Change your mindset*'. The second was that, given how effective these women were at networking, men would be mad to let gender get in the way of who they network with!

(a)   Is networking for women different than for men?

In general the feedback is that the issue is less about gender and more about developing a style for their own personality (see **Principle 2** on page 43 – '*Develop a style that works for you*'). However, they did talk about examples of where there may be differences.

"I approach both men and women in exactly the same way – professional, respectful and friendly (but not too friendly!) Unfortunately in about 35% of cases, men do not reciprocate in the same manner. I think this is a generational thing – it is older men who are more sexist. They can make personal comments, jokes, etc that are patronising and unprofessional. On these occasions, I feel as though I'm not being taken seriously. I deal very differently with these situations than when I am treated in a professional manner.

"I also find older women have a different approach than younger women (although this is a generalisation). Older women seem to be more supportive of each other, offer help and advice to each other, while younger women behave more like 'men' (i.e. more aloof, businesslike and competitive)."

Other contacts talk about how some whole industry sectors or specific companies have rather male-dominated/macho cultures. Here it can be difficult for women, unless they are prepared to fit in, which usually involves activities they may not relish, such as a lot of time at the pub or playing golf. Other industries or professions may not have a macho culture but are still dominated by men in the senior positions. As a result, it may be essential to attend events where there will be hardly any women. "Sometimes it can be awkward only because, as one of the few females in the room, you are very obvious," one contact said. But she went on to say: "Attending large network groups of all females can be just as awful as any other large group whether all male or mixed. People still stay with others they know, so breaking into little groups of people who are already engaged in conversation is just as difficult. Females can be no more welcoming to 'strangers' than males. Perhaps even less so when they find out that you won't be any use in helping them. Most men I came across were at least polite and happy to offer advice even if outside their own arena."

Some thought that they did tend to network with men and women in a different way. With men it tended to be in a more formal manner in a way that men are most used to, e.g. email contact and then meeting up by inviting them to lunch or a hospitality event. With women it tended to be more informal, e.g. by phone and then meeting up over drinks or dinner. The conversations are often quite different as well, e.g. with other women you can end up talking about the challenges of managing family and work, which is rarely a topic that is discussed with men.

(b)   What approaches can you adopt if you think that networking with the opposite sex could be awkward?
One suggestion is to meet contacts at their place of work and treat it as any other business meeting that is part of one's job. Be very clear at the start about what you are expecting from the meeting. By doing this you are much more likely to avoid the potential – real or felt – for awkward situations. The atmosphere is likely to be very different if you meet in the office rather than in a restaurant over lunch or in a bar after work. The outplacement advisor says: "Men are often such fools that, when approached by a woman, they may just try and read something else into it. So it is far better that the woman takes control of the situation." The suggestions are just as relevant for men who may feel awkward networking with women.

Other suggestions included:

At an event make a joke out of being one of the very few females. "Generally when it happened I would make some joke about being easy to spot because of being dressed in pink/green/yellow/red, anything but the ubiquitous black/grey/navy suit, i.e. noticed because of colour not my gender." Breaking the ice with a light-hearted comment is a great way to make both yourself and the person talking to you feel more comfortable. Remember that lots of men at events will be Reluctant Networkers who feel uncomfortable starting a conversation with a stranger, especially a woman; they may 'default' to talking to another man, so having some 'ice-breakers' can be really useful.

For the cases where you do not feel you are being taken seriously because you are a woman, you may have to go out of your way to 'promote' yourself by talking about your achievements and experiences, e.g. having held xyz senior position at abc (well-known) company or having run your own business, etc. You may not feel comfortable 'overselling' yourself but it may be necessary if you need to talk to someone specific. As my contact said: "If men don't take you seriously, then push your credentials hard up front and hope that it will make them change their behaviour. If it doesn't, move on – don't waste your time."

(c) What approaches work best for you?

Everybody's advice can be summarised by the principle 'Develop a style that works for you'.

Here are some of the suggestions:

♦ Some women like male company and are happy participating in activities that men typically enjoy. They may be happy to play golf or spend their evenings at the pub, but this is not for everyone. Be authentic and do what you enjoy. If you don't like golf you won't have much fun and it will show.

Putting these principles into practice

- Invest time in networking with people who meet two of the criteria in **Practical Tip 3** on page 65 – 'Focus on who you network with'. One colleague spends her networking time with business friends and former colleagues that she knows well and with whom she has enjoyed working. Although her network of men may not be that wide, the relationships she has are strong and they all know both what she is looking for and what her strengths are.

- Another one takes a similar approach: "For me the best approach is the idea of making sure to keep in touch. It is less about joining networking groups than building upon the relationships that one already has. These will be relationships built during business school, university, or through work. As these relationships become more personal and less centred on the particular work that one did together, the deeper they become. The odd email, phone call or invitation to an event or dinner are excellent ways to maintain such relationships." This approach of quality rather than quantity of relationships could be a good way for all Reluctant Networkers (regardless of gender) to start out improving their networking skills.

- Always offer to help to build a relationship. As one consultant colleague told me: "I spent quite a lot of time helping someone talk through a difficult period in their life (for both personal and professional reasons). As soon as she was back in work she gave me a project."

- "Remember networking is not selling – it is expanding your circle of professional contacts and the more you put in the more you will get out. Proactively offering to share knowledge/information or introducing someone to someone you know is much appreciated and will usually be reciprocated with helpful results."

- "Always focus on something that you are interested in rather than something you *should* be involved with – you will find it much easier to be natural and to strike up relationships."
- Avoid sectors or companies where the dominant culture does not suit you. As one consultant said about her efforts to build her contacts in one particular sector: "Join in [the drinking activities] and you lose professional credibility, don't join in and be seen as a killjoy. Eventually I decided to give up [and focus on other sectors]."
- One quote summarises their advice well: "Play to your preferences and strengths – it is important not to be one of the boys when networking with men or to behave like a man when networking with women. I think men get tired of play acting with other men and like some authentic chat that is a bit about work but a lot about good conversation and their family. Women typically don't like other pushy women or competitive conversations. In general, all sexes like to be made to feel relevant, respected and valued by others. So the usual stuff applies about asking more than telling and having a genuine interest in getting to know the person more deeply."

10 Learn from other networking styles

"Good networkers" (on page 68) are listed as one of the four groups of people on which you should focus your networking activities. You can also learn a lot from how they network. If you know any of them well enough, ask them what they think works best. Observe the 'natural' networkers at events and see what you can learn. You don't have to copy their every move (remember **Principle 2** – 'Develop a style that works for you'), just pick up a few tips and try them out for yourself.

Different nationalities tend to have different ways of networking as well. Many Americans adopt a more 'direct' approach, being quite open and up front about what they want from you. There is more emphasis on quantity rather than quality of relationships. The relationships tend to be more transactional i.e. if we can help each other out *now*, let's talk, otherwise I'm moving on to find someone else who can help me now. Remember my friend on page 42 who got two roles by being very direct and asking for them? On the right occasion it does work.

The French, on the other hand, spend more time building the personal relationship first (usually over a good lunch!), before 'doing business' with a new contact. A good example of how networking can help you make a success of your current role came from the post-merger integration role in France that I wrote about in the introduction. To find out what was really going on at our newly acquired business, I had to do a lot of 'in house' networking over lunch. This was far more effective than reading the fortnightly, official project status reports. Once I had 'invested' in getting to know my new colleagues over lunch they were much more open and honest when I needed to know the real status of each project. Networking does not have to be with people outside your company. So you can learn from both American and French styles.

11 Expect lots of no's, delays, cancellations... it's not personal... polite persistence works

"*Our greatest weakness lies in giving up. The most certain way to succeed is always to try just one more time*"
– Thomas Edison

When you are in 'job search' mode it is likely to be the single most important thing you are doing in the 'work' part of your day.

You need to recognise, however, that your need for a new job is never as important to the people you are trying to contact as it is to you. Once they have decided to offer you a job, then they will start calling you. But until then you are likely to be just another 'to do' on their task list or calendar.

In the early stages of networking when you just want to 'meet and pick their brains', you will be well down the list of priorities. Put yourself in their shoes and remember how busy you always are when you have a job. Helping other people out definitely fits into the 'nice to do' rather than the 'must do' category. Given this you should expect lots of last minute cancellations as other more important activities crop up that take precedence over seeing you. Also expect delays in responding to your calls, emails and letters.

Have some strategies for getting through to people. Personal Assistants generally control much of their bosses' diaries. Get on first name terms with them and be charming. If you encounter a PA that is not helping you get through, try calling between 5pm and 6pm or between 8am and 9am as your contact may answer the phone themselves. Often, you know the name of the person but don't have their direct email or telephone number, so you have to go through the PA. Try calling reception and saying "I'm trying to get in touch with your HR Director Alan Smith, and I have his email as asmith@newco.com – can you confirm if this is correct?" (having guessed at his/her email address…the 'Contact Us' page on a website usually tells you what comes after the @; or the Investor Relations/External Communications page for larger companies often give you somebody's email address so you can see how names are spelt e.g. asmith, a.smith, alan.smith etc). More often than not, the receptionist will confirm or correct you.

Here's another example. A friend met a contact through networking. They had a good chat but then when he tried to contact him three times over the next six months, he never had any of the calls returned. Then, after he had assumed his contact did not want to help him, he received a call from another contact asking if he was interested in a particular opportunity. The lead had come from the first contact, so maybe he had just been too busy after all.

Here is an example of spending a lot of time in 'fruitless' meetings: I wrote a 'cold call' letter to a director of a large, quoted company that would have been a great business to join. This letter led to a meeting with the Head of one department that was a complete waste of time. He could see just by reading my CV that my skills were not suited to his needs. Still, he introduced me to a more relevant colleague, who I met. He had no roles but liked me so introduced me to the Group HR Director and the head of another department. In total I met eight different people on five separate visits to this company, each time with the same response: we like you but have not got the right role for you at the moment...why not meet my colleague xyz...' The company was over 150 miles from my home. Each time it seemed like a good 'investment of my time' to take another day to develop this lead. In the end I gave up and focused on other more likely prospects. With hindsight I should either have requested another meeting only if there was a specific role available or I should have 'moved on' earlier.

The key thing to remember is that it is not personal. Before rejoining a business where I had multiple contacts at very senior levels, I went through a period of several months with no response to a number of emails and calls to several different people. I had received a job offer from them earlier in the year which had fallen through ten days before I was due to start, as it was to lead a project that had been pulled at the last minute. I had been assured that it was nothing to do with me and they were continuing to try to find another suitable role for me. I could not believe what appeared to be a 'wall of silence' and started to question whether they were serious about finding me a role. At one point I got so fed up and called up one of their major competitors and went and interviewed there.

A couple of months later I happened to be passing through London (an example of **Practical Tip 7** on page 87 – 'Find a reason to call or go and see people') and called up one of my contacts at the company and arranged to meet him. This time there were no cancellations, he came down to meet me personally in Reception and apologised profusely for not responding to my previous attempts to contact him. He even arranged for me to meet the CEO whilst I was there! Although it took another seven months for them to find me the 'right role', I left that day encouraged that it was just a question of 'when' rather than 'if' I would be offered a role. When I finally did join the company the HR Director commented that it had been like the Guinness advertising strap-line, "All good things come to those that wait" (though it had also required quite a bit of persistence as well!)

The big lesson for me was 'polite persistence'. Do not assume that because people have not returned your calls or emails they do not want to speak to you. Polite reminders in a style that work for you (see **Principle 2** on page 43) are required if you want to be an effective networker. Most people are quite happy to get gentle reminders or follow-up calls. And for the few that did not want to speak to you, the follow-up call or email has not wasted that much of your time. If you do not try, you will never know if it was just that they were too busy. But you also need to judge when to cut your losses and 'move on' to other opportunities. I tend to test these opportunities against my areas of focus (see **Practical Tip 3** on page 65 – '*Focus*')… if an opportunity fits well with my areas of focus, I'm prepared to invest more time in it.

Summary

- Keep an up-to-date database of your contacts.

- Sign up to LinkedIn (or similar networking websites) and re-connect with former colleagues who are also members.

- Join a limited number of networking groups that fit well with your goals so that you meet like-minded people and develop your contacts within your field of expertise.

- Be clear on what you want and who you network with: identify your business friends, former colleagues, decision-makers and good networkers with whom you want to focus on building your relationships.

- Use all types of means to network: email is a great networking tool, but don't use it as an excuse for not using the phone or going to meet people face-to-face. Remember that face-to-face can also be one-to-one, so spend more time in coffee shops 'catching up' with people in your network.

- Make it easy for people in your network to help you by being prepared and not putting them under pressure to say 'no'.

- You'll be amazed at how pleased former colleagues will be if you make the effort to get back in touch.

- There are lots of reasons you can develop for getting in touch with people... introducing them to other people in your network, sending interesting articles, getting them to sponsor your charity events, or just saying "I'm in your area, have you got time for a coffee?"

- If you do go to a networking event make the most of it – if you go with the right attitude you will enjoy it more than you think and get more out of it. Try and speak at an event on a subject in which you are an expert; you will not be short of people to talk to at the drinks afterwards.
- Make sure you network with both women and men.
- If you encounter a 'wall of silence' (i.e. no replies to your efforts to make contact), don't be put off. It is rare that they do not want to talk to you; it is far more likely that they are just too busy. So remember that polite persistence works.

Chapter 4:

How to get started

"Though no one can go back

and make a brand new start,

anyone can start from now and

make a brand new ending"

Carl Bard

(Scottish theologian and writer)

So far, so good, I can hear you say… I understand why networking is a good thing for me to do; I also understand the principles and can see how I could use some of the practical tips. But what do I do *now*? How do I get started? It is all rather daunting.

Personally, I can think of a number of things that I realise would be good for me to start doing, but have managed to put off actually doing for a long time. Usually they are things that I either do not know how to do or do not think I will enjoy doing (or both). I only started networking when I had to because I wanted a new job in a different sector. Then when I got the job I did not continue to network as much as I should have whilst I was in work. Now that I use networking as a key sales and marketing tool, I am sure I could do more and be more effective. When it comes to changing one's natural behaviours and bad habits, it is never easy.

"*A journey of a thousand miles begins with a single step*"
– Chinese proverb.

The best way to get started on these difficult, habit-changing activities is to break it down into 'bite-size' chunks. Spend some time developing a plan where each step is small enough and clear enough to get on with straight away. 'Start networking' is neither small nor clear. 'Write down a list of former colleagues who could be my business friends' is clear and manageable, even if time-consuming. 'Call up business friends' is not clear; you should write the name of each person individually on your list. Do not make the list so long that you never start it.

This chapter sets out some simple next steps based on the Principles and Practical Tips in the book. What you should consider doing depends somewhat on your circumstances and objectives from networking. For example you may be:

- Out of a job and looking for a new role.
- In a job where networking would make a major impact on your sales and marketing efforts e.g. running your own business where you are effectively selling your time and experience.
- In a job, working for a large company where you have little spare time and networking is a 'nice to do' rather than a 'must do' to succeed in your job.

Our needs from networking and the time we have to devote to it can be quite different:

Situation	Need from networking	Time available to network
Out of work	Immediate... you need a new job	Plenty of time
In a job requiring networking to meet key objectives	Ongoing even if not immediate... a source of new leads	Some time
In a job not requiring networking to meet key objectives	No immediate need... you have a job but want to increase your longer-term options	Hardly any spare time

1 Out of a job and looking for a new role

Principle 8 on page 55 states, '*Do it while you do not need anything*'. However, you do need something. The great thing about needing a job is that you have a lot more free time to invest in networking. So, although it is not much fun being out of full-time work, treat it as a wonderful opportunity to either build your network or revive one that is flagging, i.e. one that you have not kept live whilst you were working. When I left my manufacturing job, I had no network to speak of. I used the time in between jobs to establish my network in a way that was far quicker than had I tried to start doing it whilst in work.

You should plan to devote a significant part of your job-search time to networking in addition to following up specific job opportunities. Once you have that job, you will not get the time to go and catch up with former colleagues or meet new contacts.

Here are some 'must do' first steps. They are relatively easy to do as you do not have to make any cold calls or go and meet new people. They will probably take a fair bit of time, but it will be time well spent:

◆ Set up your database (see **Practical Tip 1** on page 61).
◆ Focus on what you want – be clear on what kind of role you want so that your network finds it as easy to help you as possible; and who you want to network with – draw up your list of contacts and follow the guidelines in this section on who can help you most e.g. decision-makers, former colleagues (see **Practical Tip 3** on page 65 – 'Focus').
◆ Research and join a *limited* number of networking websites and groups that meet your objectives (see **Practical Tip 2** on page 62); use www.linkedin.com to reconnect with former colleagues and classmates (see **Practical Tip 6** on page 83).

Now here are some of the harder next steps. You may not enjoy doing some of these (at first) but they are essential if you want to achieve any actual results from your efforts:

Call up the people on your target contact list. Start with the ones that you feel more comfortable with to get going; then once you have made a few 'easier' calls, try some harder ones; set aside some time to make a few harder ones all together. They will be easier when you are in the swing of it, rather than make one hard call a day. The key outcome of these calls is to secure a meeting.

♦ Do your preparation before the meeting (see **Practical Tip 5** on page 81).

♦ Go and see them, either at their office or go for a coffee, drink or lunch (see **Practical Tip 4** on page 80 – '*Spend more time in coffee shops*'). Remember to ask if you can help them too (see **Principle 6** on page 51).

♦ Attend the events organised by your networking group (see **Practical Tip 8** on page 88). It is better to join a limited number and then go regularly than join many and hardly attend any events. This way you start seeing a few familiar faces rather than having to deal with another roomful of strangers every time you go. You are also more likely to get help from the ones that have met you a few times than someone you meet for the first time.

♦ Repeat these steps again and again... they do become easier as you gain more practice!

And finally do not forget that once you have a job to continue to network (see **How to get started 3** on page 115).

2 Networking when your job requires it

Typically if you are in this category, it is more about improving your networking skills and activities rather than starting them.

The first steps are pretty similar to the ones in **How to get started I** on page 111:

- You probably have a database of contacts but how up to date and widespread is it? (**Practical Tip I** on page 61).
- Focus on what you are offering – be clear on what you can offer potential clients so that your network finds it as easy to help you as possible; and who you network with – draw up your list of contacts and follow the guidelines in this section on who can help you most. Have you tracked down all your former colleagues and business friends? (See **Practical Tip 3** on page 65 – '*Focus*').
- Research and join a *limited* number of networking websites and groups that meet your objectives (**Practical Tip 2** on page 62); use www.linkedin.com to reconnect with former colleagues and classmates (**Practical Tip 6** on page 83).
- Plan a regular and varied series of activities that give you a reason to get in touch with your network. These could include articles you have written, talks or lectures you are giving, events you are organising, your website upgrade or your charity fundraising activities.

Then you will need to start getting out and about and spending more time on the phone:

- Plan more time for general networking as well as following up specific leads. When was the last time you spoke or saw the people on your focus list? Can they remember what it is you do? Or maybe you have added some more strings to your bow, in which case you have a good reason to call or go and see them (see **Practical Tip 7** on page 87 – '*Find a reason to keep in touch*'). If you have not seen or spoken to them for a while, will they think of you when they hear of a lead that

could be right for you? If you want them to, you need to be
'front of mind' to coin an advertising phrase.

◆ Spend that time either on the phone or in meetings. Do not just
spend it communicating by email (**Practical Tip 4** on page 72).

◆ As well as attending networking events (See **Practical Tip
8** on page 88), volunteer to speak at them on areas of your
expertise. You may not find public speaking that easy, but talk
on a subject about which you are passionate. You will find
this much easier and will come across to your audience in the
most positive and confident way that you can. You will also not
be short of people coming up to talk to you afterwards.

◆ Organise some events for people in your network (see
Principle 8 on page 55 – '*Do it while you do not need anything*').

3   Starting to network when you are in a job

This is probably the hardest place to start improving your
networking skills. This is because most jobs these days are
getting more and more demanding, so you have less and less
spare time. Using that limited time to start doing something you
do not enjoy requires a lot of discipline. But it really is worth
making the effort. The harsh reality is that more and more
people of all levels of ability do get made redundant at some
stage of their career. Any time spent on networking whilst in
work, will help you get back into work more quickly if you do
lose your job for whatever reason. So any time spent on it is
better than nothing. Remember **Principle 8** on page 55 – '*Do it
while you do not need anything*'.

The first steps are similar to those in **How to get started 1**
and **2** on page 111 and 113, as they are about doing the groundwork
for your subsequent efforts:

- Set aside some time to network and stick to it. Use your lunch breaks or evenings. Do not be too ambitious in how much time you can devote to it at the start!
- Set up your database (**Practical Tip** I on page 61).
- Research and join a limited number of networking websites and groups that meet your objectives (**Practical Tip 2** on page 62); use www.linkedin.com to reconnect with former colleagues and classmates (**Practical Tip 6** on page 83).
- Focus on who you network with (see **Practical Tip 3** on page 65 – '*Focus on* who *you network with*'): draw up your list of contacts and follow the guidelines in this section on who can help you most. If you are not looking for a new role or project, former colleagues are a great place to start. If you are thinking about a new role you should focus on some decision-makers in that industry too. You will often get a meeting if you say that although you already have a job you are thinking about your longer-term options and so would like to get their advice. Keep your list of people to contact fairly short at the start.

Once you have done the groundwork, you will need to get communicating:
- If you are getting back in touch with former colleagues, use some time you have set aside in an early evening to make these calls. Your contacts are more likely to be available on their mobiles at that time as they may be travelling home. Even if they are in the office still they are less likely to be in a meeting. Also you may feel more comfortable calling for a general 'catch up' out of normal business hours. The purpose of these calls is to re-establish contact and catch up on how you are both getting on.

- Start with some of the 'easier' calls first, especially when you are getting back in touch with people after a long time.
- Explain why you are calling (see **Practical Tip 4** on page 72 – '*Communicate why you are communicating*'). It is OK to be honest. Just say that you are trying to get back in touch with former colleagues to improve your network. You would like to re-establish contact after all these years to find out how they are getting on and tell them what you have been up to.
- If the call goes well arrange to meet for coffee, lunch or a drink.
- Even if you do not arrange to meet, say that you hope you can stay in touch a bit more regularly now. Ensure you have their email address so that you can include them on future email updates to your network. And if they are on LinkedIn, make sure that you 'connect' with each other.
- Once you have got used to doing this, then you can start being more ambitious. Try and make contact with new people that could help you, e.g. decision-makers in your industry.

Once you have got started with this regular networking make sure you:
- Send out an annual Christmas update to your network.
- Send out an email if you have other news to tell them such as a new role within your company or at a new one.
- Tell your network if your contact details change.
- Use your network to raise extra funds for your charitable activities as well as having an excuse to contact them.

Back in **Practical Tip 4** on page 72 – '*Communicate by phone*', I talked about practising riding your bike to overcome initial fears. This came from a conversation a few years ago when someone, explaining to me about learning new skills, told me of the conscious competency model and related it to how we learn to ride a bike. The Reluctant Networker is on a similar journey based on first

The conscious competency model...

I don't know that I don't know how to ride a bicycle

I know that I don't know how to ride a bicycle

Unconscious incompetence

Conscious incompetence

...translated into the Reluctant Networker's journey...

I don't think that networking can help me

I know that networking can help me but have no idea how to go about it

You are probably somewhere here now...

realising the value of networking, taking the first few steps and then gradually improving until it becomes a much easier activity.

learning to ride a bike...

I know how to ride a bicycle but I have to concentrate	I don't even think about how to ride my bike, I just go

Conscious competence	**Unconscious competence**

I am getting better at networking but I still find it hard work	I don't even think about it, I network all the time

...keep practicing to get here!

Summary

You need to start somewhere; this will depend on what you want to get out of your networking activities:

♦ If you are out of a job, use it as an opportunity to build/refresh/extend your network as you will not have as much time to do this when you are back in work; if you do this it will be much easier to keep networking when you have landed that great new job.

♦ If you are a freelancer, you need to make sure you invest some of your time in networking, even if you are busy... it is the best way to *stay* busy as you will keep getting calls about new business.

♦ If you are busy at work set aside a small amount of time to network but don't be too ambitious... build it up gradually.

The basics for everyone:

♦ Have a database of contacts.
♦ Be clear on what you are looking for.
♦ Sign up to LinkedIn.
♦ Get communicating via a mix of email, phone and face-to-face meetings.

Chapter 5:

Why should I help? Because I can… most people are keen to help

"Life's most urgent question is:

what are you doing for others?"

Martin Luther King

(American civil rights leader)

Why should I help? Because I can...

Principle 6 on page 51 – *'It's a two-way thing'* focuses on the more selfish aspects of networking, in the sense that you never know when somebody you once helped may now help you back. There is a different approach but one that I believe many people do adopt. This is a more altruistic approach which just says, "I will help you because I can. I don't expect anything in return." For whatever reason (my seniority, experience, contacts, etc) I am in a position to help you, so I will. This may be particularly true of older, more experienced people helping younger people get started. Perhaps they are reminded of their own time when starting out and are happy to share their experiences, maybe so that others can avoid the mistakes they made. If you have a mentor, make sure you tap into their contacts as well as their experience.

When I started in my first senior general management role, I was struggling with many challenges (e.g. the huge scale of change we needed to implement, massive market pressures and only limited support from my boss); I approached a colleague who I respected and who had done a number of general management roles to act as a mentor. He was already incredibly busy with the challenges he faced in his own business. Nevertheless, I really valued the significant amount of time he gave up to help me work through some of the issues I was trying to resolve. I doubt I have done (or will do in the future) anything to repay his kindness and support and he probably knew that when he agreed to help me. Asking people in your network for some advice and maybe some contacts is not much in comparison.

There have been occasions where I have been able to help people in my network without gaining anything immediate in return. By making the right introductions I have helped people find new jobs or avoid being made redundant by finding them a role in another part of the business. I have put businesses together that have led to new customer-supplier relationships. I have helped people get over the initial shock of being made redundant and not knowing how to start networking to find a new role. I have done this by talking them through my own experiences and showing them a draft of this book. In each case, I have really enjoyed helping them, even though there was no tangible benefit to me, apart from having a few more people that 'owed me one'.

So I want to end on an uplifting note. Never underestimate the willingness of most people to help 'because they can'. You just need to ask and make it easy for them. With networking it is often hard to distinguish between altruism and acting selfishly. Some ancient religions believe in a version of karma – 'what goes around, comes around'. They believe that if you do a good deed to someone, they are likely to do a good deed themselves, probably not back to you but to someone else; that person then does a good deed themselves and so on, until one day someone does a good deed back to you. As the native American Betty Laverdure said, "Everything's a circle. We're each responsible for our actions. It will come back."

So go on, get started today and give yourself more options for a successful and enjoyable career. What are you waiting for?

"Better to do something imperfectly than to do nothing flawlessly"
– Robert Schuller (US pastor and author)

References

7 Habits of Highly Effective People by Stephen R Covey
(Simon and Schuster, 2004)

*Now, Discover Your Strengths: How to Develop Your Talents
and Those of the People You Manage*
by Marcus Buckingham and Donald O Clifton
(Pocket Books, New edition, 2005)

Alice's Adventures in Wonderland by Lewis Carroll

*What Color is Your Parachute? 2000: A Practical Manual
for Job-hunters and Career-changers* by Richard N Bolles
(Ten Speed Press, 1999)

The Elephant and the Flea: Looking Backwards to the Future
by Charles Handy (Arrow Books, 2002)

*From New Recruit to High Flyer: No-nonsense Advice on
How to Fast Track Your Career* by Hugh Karseras
(Kogan Page, 2006)

Brand You: Turn Your Unique Talents into a Winning Formula
by John Purkiss and David Royston-Lee
(Artesian Publishing, 2009)

The Future of Careers
by Roffey Park Institute/Linda Holbeche (2000)

Getting a Job: A Study of Contacts and Careers
by Mark Granovetter
(The University of Chicago Press, 1995)